# THEY HATE IF YOU'RE CLEVER AND DESPISE A FOOL

## *RACE AND CLASS: A view from the bottom up*

by: Valeriano Diviacchi

*They hurt you at home and they hit you at school*
*They hate if you're clever and despise a fool*
*Till you're so fucking crazy you can't follow their rules*
*A working class hero is something to be*

**Working Class Hero**
Ozzy Osbourne

TABLE OF CONTENTS

Page


I.     Preface / Personal Motivation for this Book     1

II.    Prologue: The Death of History is not the End of History    13

    A.    Let's Kill History    16

        1)    *There is too much of it.*    17

        2)    *It has no predictive value.*    19

        3)    *No one who is anyone cares about history except for the power to make history.*    21

        4)    *Normative values really do negate history.*    22

        5)    *Its death may be better in the long run because workers are much better at storytelling.*    24

    B.    Propaganda    34

    C.    History and "the problem of the color-line"    35

III.    IS A "SOCIAL CONSTRUCT" A SOCIAL CONSTRUCT OR AN ONTOLOGY?    43

    A.    What are social constructs and what is ontologically a fact?    47

    B.    The Practical difference Between a Social Construct and an Ontological Fact Is One of Degrees of Pragmatic Value and Not of Substance.    54

IV.    THE PRAGMATIC NECESSITY OF CLASS    59

Page

V.     WHAT IS RACE?     71

      A.    The Problem of Rachel Dolezale and the Answer
It Gives to My Question    79

VI.    ANALYSIS / THE RELATIONSHIP BETWEEN
RACE AND CLASS – PRESENT AND FUTURE    91

      A.    Race in the Present    93

      B.    The Future of Race    96

      C.    The Present of Class    101

      D.    The Future of Class    108

VII.    RACE, CLASS, LAW, EDUCATION, AND ETHICS    115

VIII.    CONCLUSION    123

EPILOGUE    125

BIBLIOGRAPHY    129

*Of all tyrannies, a tyranny sincerely exercised for the good of its victims may be the most oppressive. It would be better to live under robber barons than under omnipotent moral busybodies. The robber baron's cruelty may sometimes sleep, his cupidity may at some point be satiated; but those who torment us for our own good will torment us without end for they do so with the approval of their own conscience.*

— C. S. Lewis

# I.     PREFACE / PERSONAL MOTIVATION FOR THIS ESSAY

I appreciate this opportunity to reach some semblance of finality in my lifelong contemplations of race and class with some final readings and to write up my conclusions. Thus, as this Preface title implies, part of this essay will be more personal contemplation than a scholarly one; there will be personal facts included in this contemplation in addition to the other empirical reality contemplated. I was tempted to make this a memoir *a la* the book *Hillbilly Elegy* written by J.D. Vance. Vance after completing the simple-minded task of graduating Yale Law decided to set his life and career on a firm foundation (that is, a big law firm foundation representing the rich and powerful) by telling rich people what they want to hear about the *hoi polloi* he left behind. But, what I want to say is neither what those in power nor the *hoi polloi* what to hear. The reality is that Vance's simple view that success is due to the choices one makes just as his compatriot black writer Ta-Nehisi Coates' converse message that failure means one is a victim of structure are both wrong. Success and failure are defined by social class reality not by any individual traits, skill, or work. As soon as any individual especially one not born to class privilege accepts such reality, the better and happier their life will be including if their life is one of struggle and rebellion against that reality as mine has been.

According to post-modern social justice theory, I must include my personal life in any analysis anyway because it is my subjective perspective that creates a fictional "empirical reality" they must deconstruct to get the real story of what I am saying. Supposedly any empirical reality I describe is really fiction created by my personal will to power. Fine, but I will keep my personal life to the minimum necessary for my contemplations. Anyone who disagrees with my analytic conclusions will no doubt be quick to point out my personal flaws anyway.

The nature of race is something I have been contemplating ever since I witnessed my first acts of old school racial hatred in grammar school in the much more violent world of my youth. In that world, racial hatred was one of many hatreds common and intermixed with a wide variety of many other hates varying from ethnic rivalries going back centuries and some a millennium or so and onto daily newly born street gang territorial disputes. Unlike most who whine about it, I have actually looked into the eyes of someone trying to kill me for who "I am" and not simply imagined it. However, as I will contemplate in this essay, there is a material difference in the hate of old school racism and present new school racism. At least, in the old world of my youth, we were acting innocently out of passion and ignorance; present racists and the intellectuals and others who profit from them are acting rationally and from intentional delusion.

I recently read a speech given by Michelle Obama, a classmate of mine from Harvard Law (my only claim to fame), at a Tuskegee University commencement part of which states:

> Instead they will make assumptions about who they think you are based on their limited notion of the world. My husband and I know how frustrating that experience can be. We've both felt the sting of those daily slights throughout our entire lives — the folks who crossed the street in fear of their safety; the clerks who kept a close eye on us in all those department stores; the people at formal events who assumed we were the "help" — and those who have questioned our intelligence, our honesty, our love of this country.[1]

As she was a Princeton graduate, she was out of my league and not even an acquaintance of mine at law school. From my few contacts with her I do remember her as a good person and no doubt she is but given the naivete of this speech, I am very glad she never came to my neighborhood when growing up. Rich white people including those who are black might "fear" black people and cross the street to avoid them but not in my neighborhood.

---

[1]

https://obamawhitehouse.archives.gov/the-press-off
ice/2015/05/09/remarks-first-lady-tuskegee-universi
ty-commencement-address

If she or her future husband had come to my neighborhood, people would not fearfully cross the street. Instead, many would confront them for being on their street; tell them to leave; and physically threaten them if they did not. Often those threats were carried out. Racism does not involve fearing blacks or any race, it involves hating them. Growing up, I wished that greasers and ethnic bigots would have had crossed the street when they saw me, it would have made my life easier.

Based on my life experience and reading of history, fear by the oppressor of the oppressed is a good thing; it gives the oppressed leverage on their oppressors. Individuals may sometimes altruistically help others, but societies and those who rule them never do so.

Class is something I have been contemplating on and off since high school. It was at that time that my illiterate laborer and cleaning woman immigrant parents were able to scrap the money together to pay for my tuition to the college preparatory Fenwick High School about which I had learned purely as a coincidence given it was outside my working class neighborhood and into which I had been able to test. Michelle Obama is insulted when "the people at formal events ... assumed we were the 'help'". Well, I and my family were and I still am the help. Despite my present Harvard degree and my having worked my whole life to become "the people at formal events", I still am the help, and I am socially treated as the help including by corporate lawyers like Michelle Obama. I do not consider it anything of which to be ashamed as she apparently does. High school was my introduction to this conceptual reality in which not only should I be ashamed but that I should be ashamed for not being ashamed for being the help:

> Let me tell you about the very rich. They are different from you and me. They possess and enjoy early, and it does something to them, makes them soft, where we are hard; cynical where we are trustful; in a way that, unless you were born rich, it is very difficult to understand.[2] — F. Scott Fitzgerald.

These contemplations took a break during my military service after

---

[2] Fitzgerald, F. Scott and Matthew J. Bruccoli, ed. *The Short Stories of F. Scott Fitzgerald*, "The Rich Boy". New York: Scribner's (1989). p. 335.

high school in the Submarine Service of the United State Navy. The clarity
of living in what is by necessity an openly structured social hierarchy in the
military especially aboard a warship at sea was not conducive to
contemplating and especially not to questioning any social hierarchy because
doing so would get you into serious trouble — as it eventually did. Initially,
however, I welcomed the clarity of the military structured hierarchy as a
relief from the chaos and anarchy that was my life up to enlistment.
Unfortunately, to this day, the military is the closest to a meritocracy I have
experienced in life which is more of a comment on the random and arbitrary
nature of the civilian world than it is a compliment of the military. As
miserable as it was, the submarine service gave me the only sense of
community I have ever known — another sad comment on the civilian world.
It was not "love of country" that motivated us and kept us going through the
misery but a sense of duty to ourselves and our shipmates. The advantage of
military service for those who do not take it as a career to become lifers is
learning its patriotism is as much a first refuge as it a last refuge for
scoundrels (to paraphrase Samuel Johnson).

My contemplation of class reignited and burned with a higher
intensity after my honorable discharge when eventually after graduating from
the University of Illinois Chicago using the G.I.Bill, I started my studies at
Harvard Law School. There, despite everything I had accomplished and
worked hard to overcome in my life all of which was more physically and
intellectually challenging than the mind-numbing academics of the law, I
came the closest to committing suicide because of its social challenges that I
could not overcome and knew I would never overcome — that I have still not
overcome to this day nor ever will. I was born immigrant white trash and will
die so, regardless of my Ivy League degree and other successes in life. I will
always be known by my failures — as I should be known. By the necessary
law of nature known as class struggle and as I will honestly admit should be
the case for anyone trying to go above their born class in life without selling
their soul to get there, attempts to win class struggle should not be rewarded
by the Powers-that-be. Unless one is willing to sell one's soul for the power
of ruling or to the rulers, one should not be ruling. The present ruling class
ideology called the law loves poor and oppressed victims as long as they stay
poor and oppressed victims.

For the Harvard elite or anyone to have accepted me into their world
would have been and still would be a horrible mistake. Just as was true for
the Spartans and Romans in their respective Republics, the last thing the
United States needs is a helot or plebeian with political power. It is one thing
to have pretend revolutions such as *Occupy Wall Street, Black Lives Matter,*

*Alt-Right,* and former corporate lawyer Michelle Obama virtue-signaling with cardboard signs while the Powers-that-be go about their business; but, as I will contemplate further, having someone like me among them would be the pincer movement for all sorts of grief and destruction that for the good of my beloved United States must not occur.

For example, during the Great Depression, the white trash working class hero Senator Huey Long of Louisiana proposed a law making it illegal for anyone to earn more than $1 million a year and for anyone to inherit more than $5 million. Adjusting for inflation, that would presently be about $15 million a year and inheritances at about $75 million. He was assassinated shortly thereafter. Rightly so for making such a proposal, as I should be when — if I ever were to get the power — I would propose anarchy as my opening ante in the ruling class game of politics. Instead, the Depression gave us the patrician Franklin D. Roosevelt who after applying enough band aids to the economy to save capitalism from the labor movement striking and fighting it on a daily basis finally ended the Great Depression by getting us involved in World War II. After my ante, my opening bet in the normative wordgames of politics and the law would be to call their bluff and to require all schools including private universities such as NYU and Harvard to maintain a student body that matched economically the available student population. So, since 20% of children in the Unites States live in poverty[3], 20% of the student body would have to be from below the poverty line and so forth. What a culture shock that would be! Almost as bad for the professors as my first six months as a student were at Harvard Law. Ivy League professors and colleges would actually have to start teaching and dealing with real diversity of students and opinion instead of the pretend diversity in which all students regardless of race, ethnicity, sex, and so forth are acceptable as long as they act, speak, and have the same acceptable beliefs. I would be assassinated multiple times — and should be.

However, I want to emphasize this essay is not intended to be a condemnation of the past nor of the present. The world is a much better place now quantitatively then it ever has been in history. There is no such thing as the good old days. However, they were not the bad old days either. They just were and are now gone just as our present days will also be gone some day. The modern habit of condemning the past and the dead, as I will contemplate further, is an attribute of the arrogance and laziness of modern intelligentsia

---

[3]

http://www.nccp.org/topics/childpoverty.html

and their worshipers enjoying the luxury and comfort created for them by the struggles of generations of our unknown and uncountable ancestors upon whom they metaphorically spit as if they would have done better. Approximately 100 billion individuals have lived, struggled in life, and died to give us our present reality of approximately six billion souls on earth: about 15 ghosts for each of us.[4] The post-modernist or any social justice dogma seeing these 15 ghosts as all ignorant evil fools manipulated by evil racists or "Whiteness" in which there is no progress in history is one of their biggest ongoing frauds. Despite two World Wars in the 20th Century, human population went from proximately 1.5 billion in 1900 to more than six billion at the end of the 20th Century.[5] Most of these six billion are living on average the longest, most materially rich, and healthiest lives of any humans in history. Just in my lifetime, a time of omnipresent violence and hatred in the world in which I grew up and which I find hard to believe I survived has transformed into one of the most peaceful ages known to history.[6] Every indication is that this progress will continue, maybe.

There is a whole universe out there waiting to be discovered, explored, and conquered; sure would be fun to do it or have one of my descendants do it.

There is one danger to this historical quantitative progress continuing, the fact that qualitatively human nature has not changed while it is now dealing with the new historical Powers-that-be of a Technological Society[7]. The advantage of physical violence and hate is its clarity; growing up, I always knew who my enemies were and who my friends were. This is no longer true of the modern world in which soon all violence will be

---

[4] Stephenson, Wesley. "Do the Dead Outnumber the Living?". *BBC News.* http://www.bbc.com/news/magazine-16870579

[5] https://en.wikipedia.org/wiki/World_population

[6] *See generally* Gat, Azar. *War in Human Civilization.* Oxford University Press: Oxford (2006).

[7] Ellul, Jacques. *The Technological Society.* Vintage Books: N.Y., N.Y. (1964).

intellectual, rationalized, and disguised as ethics and morality — nonphysical passive/aggressive violence enforced by the monopoly on actual physical violence that is the law and the ruling class ideology it enforces. "Physical rebellion, or any preliminary move towards rebellion, is at present not possible"[8] and will not be for the foreseeable future. Despite quantitative progress, qualitatively neither humanity nor individual humans have changed. As best summarized by George Orwell:

> By comparison with that existing today, all the tyrannies of the past were half-hearted and inefficient. ... Part of the reason for this was that in the past no government had the power to keep its citizens under constant surveillance. The invention of print, however, made it easier to manipulate public opinion, and the film and the radio carried the process further. With the development of television and the personal computer, and the technical advances which made it possible to receive and transmit simultaneously on the same instrument, private life came to an end. Every citizen, or at least every citizen important enough to be worth watching, could be kept for twenty-four-hours a day under the eyes of the police and in the sound of official propaganda, with all other channels of information closed. The possibility of enforcing not only complete obedience to the will of the State, but complete uniformity of opinion on all subjects, now existed for the first time.[9]  — George Orwell, *1984*.

In this essay, I will contemplate a conceptual analysis similar to that done by Amy Gutmann and Kwame Anthony Appiah in their book *Color Conscious: The Political Morality of Race.* As a book written respectively by the President and head of the philosophy department of the world universities that are respectively the University of Pennsylvania and NYU, I will be referencing to this book as an exemplification of the present supposedly non-racist conceptualization of race and class by Western intelligentsia and by the "intellectual proletariat" as Thomas Sowell calls those who presently dominate the normative control of these concepts just as they did at the turn of the 20th Century when their conceptualization of race was clearly racist

---

[8] Orwell, George. *1984*. Signet Classics Penguin Group: NY, NY (1977). p. 210.

[9] Orwell, George. *1984*. p. 205-210.

and either nonexistent or Marxist regarding class [10]. Thus, for reasons I will argue, such as the death of history, this essay will be substantively more conceptual and analytic than empirical.

I do not consider this limitation to concept analysis to be a weakness. Empirical questions must be examined and decided empirically, however as modern philosophy has undisputedly shown to be the case, such examination and decision are theory laden. Purely conceptual questions regarding those theories such as their logic, their logical and structural relationships, and thus whether they are anything more than aesthetics are the province of philosophical contemplation. If such conceptual questions are ignored, we end up with a world of nonsense not only without knowing it is nonsense but without having a language for discussing the nonsense.

"Any attempt to have rational discourse requires that those with different views have a common language ..."[11] Because Western Civilization is now a Technological Society using mathematical wordgames in which the humanities only play a normative role, this common language is missing. In fact, they are in conflict; rational thought in the humanities is now always reversed: rationalization of experience comes before the experience they seek to rationalize.[12] Experience in the humanities is not just theory laden, it is just theory — theory that gives only aesthetic value yet through law is enforced by a monopoly on violence. Because of the material power of the modern world, we are now free to believe what we want including to ignore reality and then use these voluntary or involuntary beliefs as rules of conduct to create morality and ethics. In more primitive times, such power to ignore reality would have killed us. Now, delusion no longer kills us but gives meaning to our lives. In our present world and for the foreseeable future, it is a matter of normative reality that it is impossible to talk about race and class unless those talking agree on their analytic conceptual meanings first; the conceptual battle lines have been drawn and a no prisoners and no retreat battle plan instituted so it is impossible to cross the lines either by or for

---

[10] Sowell, Thomas. *Intellectuals and Race.* Basic Books: NY, NY (2013). pp. 46, 47, 48.

[11] Sowell, Thomas. *Intellectuals and Race.* p. 3.

[12] Ellul, Jacques. *The Technological Society*; Sowell, Thomas. *Intellectuals and Race.*

empirical problem solving. "[M]oral character and ethics matter more than science"[13] was the call to arms by which University of Illinois associate professor Kate Clancy successfully dis-invited  James Watson, a Nobel laureate who in 1953 co-discovered the double-helix structure of DNA with Francis Crick and Rosalind Franklin, from speaking at the University of Illinois. At present and for the foreseeable future, especially with the death of history, any empirical decisions as to whether race or class have any scientific predictive meaning are predetermined by the conceptual norms of those who decide what empirical research will be done and who will do it. Thus, I will concentrate on an analytic contemplation of those conceptual norms: their use and usefulness which are their meaning.

I will begin my contemplation with the concept of history and how it has become irrelevant to any discussion or contemplation of class and race except for understanding why it is irrelevant. History is dead, however the death of history does not mean the end of history. Within small communities, storytelling is replacing history, especially fiction through visual means such as short digital media that is becoming the dominant tool for transmitting a social reason for being. In the larger society, for power crossing all classes, propaganda has become and will be the dominant tool for creating reasons for being and for history.

I will then contemplate the difference between the concepts of a social construct and of an ontology that also go by other names such as social kinds and natural kinds; existentialism and essentialism; nature and nurture; realism and phenomenalism; and many more trying to differentiate between words that represent a human creation dependent upon our existence and words that represent an entity independent of out existence. I will argue that in modern ontology, such differentiations are a matter of degree and not of any substantive importance. The concept of a "social construct" is itself ontology. Ultimately, as the philosopher Willard V.O. Quine[14] argued

---

[13] Clancy, Kate. Twitter tweet at http://secondlanguage.blogspot.com/2017/05/kate-c lancy-gets-james-watson-disinvited.html

[14] Quine, Willard V.O. "On What There Is". *Review of Metaphysics* (1948). Reprinted in 1953 *From a Logical Point of View*. Harvard University Press. https://pdfs.semanticscholar.org /05f2/9bb9be63647f8897775461c18e96026cec20.p

generally, the ontology of race and class as is all knowledge is holistic, they cannot be seen as existing independently of each other but as an intertwined fabric of acts and power. For an understanding of race and class as concepts, we must have some logical consistency: 1) what one's ontology logically requires to exist must be admitted to exist; 2) any overlapping of logically required existence by opposing ontology must be admitted to exist by both.

Of course, one is free to reject the principle of non-contradiction and argue that logical consistency is itself a social construct that can be rejected if normatively necessary. Fine, I can live with that and the resulting anarchy of contradictory norms. The problem is that those that argue for such rejection usually cannot, but instead are the most hypocritical in the enforcement of their morality and ethics by usually the principle of contradiction to argue and enforce them. It is basic logic that arguing from false premises and contradiction allows for proof of anything and for believing anything to be true. Such anarchy describes the life of most working class surviving on passion and a will to live and thus I can deal with it; however, I do not see those who advocate a rejection of classical logic as accepting the reality of the anarchy that rationally follows. One cannot go around complaining about racism or making any other claims that "moral character and ethics matter" while saying that anything goes. If anything goes then anything goes, all norms including morality become a battle of wills for power not of "moral character and ethics matter more than science". Thus, "matter more" means "want more".

My arguments will lead to the following conclusions: 1) concepts such as race and class exist in a holistic fabric of knowledge in which the difference between a social construct and an ontological reality is one of degree of pragmatic value not of substance thus they can be and are both at the same time; 2) the concept of race is presently a concept serving many uses that are most useful as an industry to give meaning and material wealth to the lives of those who control its normative use thus creating a new school form of racism that can only be eliminated by technology and not by any social dialogue or constructs because new school racism needs victims for its norms as much as it needs masters for its norms; 3) class defines the degree by which any individual in a social group or by which subgroups of individuals in a social group have the power to control the normative language of the entire group — it is the power to decide what the entire

---

df

group normatively ought to be or do; 4) class is an ontological reality in any human social structure including Western Civilization that has so far been able to control class to its benefit but may not be able to do so in the near future; 5) The nature of present Technological Society more than ever needs social class struggle as a necessary ontological reality to maintain historical material progress regardless of social justice pretensions to the contrary.

# PROLOGUE: THE DEATH OF HISTORY IS NOT THE END OF HISTORY

*A man thinks that by mouthing hard words he understands hard things.*

— Herman Melville

I am taking the definition of history for purposes of this essay to be the written study, examination, and analysis of narratives or sequences of past events to examine and analyze them in order objectively to describe them and patterns in those events. The key problem here is "objectively". Even if anyone wanted to believe in objective historical analysis anymore, it is simply not practically possible to do so any more — assuming it ever was.

There is much history to learn, question, argue, and dispute concerning race and class. At present and for the foreseeable future, the most bitter disputes deal with race and racism that from the perspective of a history nerd such as me should be treated both factually and conceptually as history and historical analysis, but it is impossible to do so. It is impossible to have a meaningful factual dispute on race and racism because the concept of "objectively" has lost meaning in any rational disputes other than in hard science because of the proliferation of the concept of "social construct" and its progeny that I will contemplate in the next section. Even in hard science, objective meaning is subject to doubt. If the Nobel Prize winner James Watson and the distinguished Black historian Thomas Sowell cannot discuss history without being called respectively a racist and an Uncle Tom, an old white guy like me must be racist and cannot be objective on any race or racism questions despite being married to a black woman and thus having a black daughter as most people would characterize her. History no longer provides a common language for any disputes involving history. We need to contemplate race and class without it, but only after we understand why it is dead and why I argue it is good it is dead.

The big question is will propaganda replace history or has it already?

In his book *The Killing of History,* the historian Keith Windschuttle conducts, as other old school historians have tried in the last couple of decades, a valiant defense against the post-modernist and now social justice analysis of history and classical historical scholarship as simply fiction written and created by historians as myth to support and hide the social self-interest of the powerful. Windschuttle describes how academia through structuralism, post-structuralism, modernism, post-modernism, and now social justice theory has convinced much of the intelligentsia, their students, and the public that history is not an empirical bearer of truth and an inheritance of wisdom but is fiction that needs to be deconstructed to reveal the hidden self-interest and will to power intentions of those that write it. According to present social justice theory, we can only learn history and understand "the Other" by listening to fictional stories and storytelling. It is called storytelling, but is it really propaganda? How do they get away with deconstructing all history with which they disagree as fiction by using arguments based on their own statement of history and historical analysis? If all history is fiction, is not the history they cite to support their argument that history is fiction also fiction?

Though I fully agree with Windschuttle's desperate attempt at defending history from its attackers in the finest traditions of Thermopylae, it is a rear guard action that unlike the Battle will not eventually lead to victory. The fact that social justice theory uses argument based on its empirical conclusions about the past to support its conclusions should be a sufficient rational basis in itself to defeat its conclusions, but such would only be true if social justice warriors were to accept the principle of non-contradiction as a sound and necessary basis for argument, something it and its practitioners do not. It was realistic for him to end his book by citing possible saviors of history to be historians such as John Clive whose "Clive thesis" argues for historians to make their writings more art than fact and to treat "history as literature".[15] No need for that thesis anymore. There is no shortage of artists. What are rare and soon to be nonexistent are historians willing to write hundreds and even thousands of pages of critical thought by narrative with supporting facts and who have the imagination, creativity, and life experience to read the details so as to synthesize and transform those facts into both empathy for the dead and for their dead world in order to create a rational understanding of a live world. However, as history teaches, there is no stopping an idea whose time or whose death has come.

Though I do not agree with post-modern social justice theory analysis that history is fiction needing to be replaced by storytelling, as much as it pains me to say it, for practical reasons it might as well be or soon will be. Thus I and anyone contemplating race and class in the present world and its foreseeable future need to get on with the contemplation without relying

---

[15] Windschuttle, K. *The Killing of History.* Encounter Books: NY, NY (1996). pp. 268-78.

much, if any, on history for any premises or conclusions.

Some contemplation of history is necessary to understand why it is dead, is immaterial to present arguments on race, and to counteract the reliance on history by post-modernism to argue we should not rely on history. Thus, I will for these reasons include some history including my personal history in this contemplation. However, in the end, historical argument will not resolve present disputes on race and class.

As I stated before, this is not meant as whining for the good old days. History when we had it did not do us in the working and lower classes much good though the little it did materially changed us human society — for the good and bad.

## A.      <u>Let's Kill History</u>

Even at the early stages of any contemplation of race and class, there is an initial instinct to contemplate class and race through history but this temptation must be resisted. History is dead not for any theoretical "deconstruction" reasons but for very practical reasons:

1)       there is too much of it;

2)       it has no predictive value;

3)       no one who is anyone cares about history except for the power to make history;

4)       normative values really do negate history;

5)       its death may be better in the long run for workers and the poor because we are much better at storytelling than those who advocate storytelling.

Historically, history involved a Quinean intertwined fabric of knowledge involving individual acts and social forces. It is this holistic complexity that makes history in a world of discrete data bits, sound bites, digital media, and tweets worthless for rational argument. Furthermore, for purposes of starting and maintaining any class struggle against racism or a ruling class, its death is not to be regretted. This is so not because of social justice hypocritical and contradictory conceptual rejections of history, but simply because of practical reality.

<u>*1)*</u>     ***There is too much of it.***

The last history book I was able to read before starting my NYU studies was *Napoleon: Soldier of Destiny* by Michael Broers. Great book if you have time to read about 900 pages in paperback — covering only up to the French Revolution, the Haitian Revolution, and the first half of Napoleon's Regime as this book is the first of two volumes. I am awaiting publication of volume two though I doubt I will have time to read it. As even Windschuttle had to admit, "[a]nyone who buys a history book to read (rather than to decorate the bookshelf) is making a commitment to a long and sustained engagement with it"[16]. Having the time for such commitment is the first problem; picking the subject of such commitment in a complex world of globalization involving holistic knowledge is the second problem. If one is going to spend hours on a history book, why Napoleon? Why not Joshua, Themistocles, Qin Shi Huang, Marcus Agrippa, Flavius Belisarius, or Khalid ibn al-Walid whose military conquests gave us the Muslim World and its problems for us? Why limit it to military generals, why not read about common soldiers such as *A Long Way Gone* by Ishmael Beal (good book) and many more? What about non-military events such as international economic history? Though the history of the world may be the history of war, there is much other history. Almost all popular factual opinion about any major historical event ranging from the Assassination of President Kennedy to World War II and most certainly about the history of slavery is factually wrong, but it took me years of reading opposing histories on the same events to understand they are wrong. Since the time of Thucydides, considered by most historians as the founder of their profession and of the concept of realist history, historians have always written for and been read by the few with the knowledge, time, and need to read it; most of society survived upon myth, stories, tales, rumor, propaganda, and fake news even before we had the words "fake news". In our Technological Society, those with the intellect and need to read history not only no longer have the necessary time to read it, they do not want to read it. When they do read it, they read only the history that will confirm their pre-existing opinions about history — reading propaganda is easier.

I was hoping that data science would provide some type of resolution

---

[16] Windschuttle, K. *The Killing of History.* p. 275.

to this problem. Its ability to use computer power to correlate billions and soon trillions and quadrillion pieces of data in short amounts of time seemed like a solution to getting some understanding of the vast amounts of history now available as information, but it turns out I am wrong. Data science is used and is useful to provide solutions to a problem presented to it as defined by human algorithms but there is no understanding or even explanation as to why the solution works to solve the problem. There is nothing wrong with this reality[17] and for the foreseeable future it is the best science can do, but history without understanding or explanation is simply an infinitely large file cabinet with infinite records for which a computer lacks an algorithm to correlate; the understanding or explanation needed to write the algorithm is somewhere in the file cabinet. It is similar to having an answer on a password-protected computer but not knowing the password.

---

[17] Diviacchi, V. "Knowledge and Truth in Data Science: Theory without Theory". https://papers.ssrn.com/sol3/papers.cfm?abstract_id =3091356

<u>**2)**</u>     <u>***It has no predictive value.***</u>

Any critical analysis of history will have to admit: history does not generally repeat itself. One can learn much from history, such as an understanding of the lives of the 15 ghosts for each of us whose struggles created our world if one is open to gaining such empathy, but that is about it. In our Technological Society, truth is defined by predictive value and meaning as it should be. From the moment we are conceived, nature is trying to kill us; we need to know what predictively works in order to survive. Predictive meaning requires using mathematics to quantify information as data to create probabilities for future events. A file cabinet full of records that cannot be quantified has no predictive meaning.

Historical facts however do have significant aesthetic value if one has the power to pull whatever facts one needs from history to support one's normative arguments as is the case with all arguments on race and class. One can find in history facts to support any belief no matter how ridiculous. The Party slogan "[w]ho controls the past, ... controls the future, ... who controls the present controls the past" is dependent not on predictive meaning but on the ability to pull from history and to insert its facts as needed into normative arguments to give aesthetic support to whatever future the Party intends to create; it does not depend on predictive value.[18] Predictive value is dependent on something working to actually solve a problem, but aesthetic meaning has no such handicap. For example, if one creates the description *"F=ma"* and uses inputs to describe predictively answers but miscalculates when sending a rocket to the moon, your intention to reach the moon will fail. If one normatively states what *"F=ma"* ought to be and then one ignores it when attempting to send a rocket to the moon because one normatively concludes *"F"* ought not be a certain value because it is evil or it is good that rockets cannot go to the moon, the resulting failure is still normatively true in relation to your normative statement regardless of whether the rocket makes it to the moon or not. This is why the dystopia of Orwell's *1984* and realities such as North Korea can last as long as their human population continues to reproduce and there is no foreign opposition — pragmatic success does not matter to ethics or morality. Failure can be a good and success bad in ethics and morality.

As the philosopher David Hume established centuries ago known as

---

[18] Orwell, George. *1984*. p. 34.

Hume's Law or Hume's Guillotine, there is no logical relationship between what is and what ought to be. The work of intelligentsia especially of all law school intelligentsia is aimed at being the wizard behind the smokescreen they generate to hide this reality of their ideology. "Chemists or chess grandmasters may be of equal or greater mental accomplishments, but they are not intellectuals because their work ends with an outcome subject to empirical verification by known standards, while the outcomes of the work of intellectuals are subject essentially to peer consensus."[19]

---

[19] Sowell, Thomas. *Intellectuals and Race.*

No-one-that-is-anyone with the power to decide in any given situation what normatively ought to be cares about history or descriptive patterns in history, nor is there any reason they should. Power lies not in describing and understanding history but in making history in one's image as the gods or God does. Early in world history and on to the recent past, Powers-that-be varying from the Ancients to recent Caesars such an Adolf Hitler and Winston Churchill and similar Powers needed some understanding of history to gain power but the understanding necessary lessened more and more as we proceeded into Technological Society. As extensively written by Jacques Ellul in *The Technological Society* and by George Orwell in *1984*, we have reached a point in which technology gives a few the power to create their own world without concern for the past, future, or the present. Technicians and their technology are now available — doing Winston's job in *1984* — to the few with the desire and power to make history by creating whatever past or present history is needed to achieve future power.

Furthermore, success is achieved solely by obtaining power not by doing anything with it. Winston's epiphany finally came when he realized "GOD IS POWER"[20]. "The Party seeks power entirely for its own sake"[21]; power is an end in itself. Orwell and Ellul reached the same conclusions by different paths. Orwell's *1984* goes from flaws in human nature and its class struggle to conclude power becoming an end in itself; Ellul argues the technology we have created will exacerbate flaws in human nature so that power becomes an end in itself.

Both Ellul and Orwell as with many philosophers see the proverbial end of history in Technological Society. Nonsense, the death of history is not the end of history nor of life.

---

[20] Orwell, George. *1984*. p. 277.

[21] Orwell, George. *1984*. p. 263.

I ridicule Professor Kate Clancy in her refusal to listen to a knowledgeable scientist regarding his science simply because she does not believe he is a good person, but really in the end she got what she wanted just as those with normative power, that is with the power to say and enforce what "ought to be" in any given situation, will always win out in the end if there is no opposing power. This reality is not necessary a bad thing. For example, chattel slavery was seen as an ethical good throughout human history in every human culture from the lowest "indigenous" or whatever tribe onto the most powerful civilizations. Slaves were present both in Plato's *Republic* and in Thomas Moore's *Utopia*. The unfortunate reality is that slavery worked to help our ancestors survive and to prosper under physical and mental stresses I doubt most modern humans can even imagine. At present, the millennial generation seems to consider bullying and name-calling as types of ultimate evil; it is hard — for me at least — to imagine such a generation dealing with hordes of rampaging, pillaging, and invading military nomads coming down from the steppes on a regular basis to rampage, pillage, and invade. How about instead of Uber, one had to walk everywhere — I mean everywhere. If something unfortunate happens in the future, such as the volcano caldron that is Yellowstone National Park erupting and putting us all back into the Stone Age, I suspect the Powers who survive will fairly quickly realize that chattel slavery can be as ethical a means to survive as they did in the past — just as they see no problem with wage slavery now. There is nothing in history that would serve as an argument to stop them. Unless there exists the moral strength independent of history to defeat a historical ethical argument for chattel slavery, there will be a return of chattel slavery.

In the 5$^{\text{th}}$ Century A.D., when the Roman patrician Saint Melaine, a member of the ancient well-established patrician Roman Valerii Family who owned property and between 50,000 and 100,000 slaves on real estate holdings scattered from Britannia to Southern Italy and onto Roman North Africa, converted to Christianity she freed her personal eight thousand slaves. What did the freed slaves do? Many of the liberated slaves volunteered to be slaves with her brother from whom they expected employment and protection.[22] Often in life, moral strength is more important than history both for the moral and the immoral, especially given that ethics historically is never able to differentiate between the moral and immoral.

------------------------------

[22] Wolfgram, Herwig. *The Roman Empire and its Germanic Peoples*. n. 39 at pp. 57-58. U. of CA. Press, 1993.

<u>**5)**</u>       ***Its death may be better in the long run because workers are much better at storytelling.***

For the above listed practical reasons, history is dead and myth is reborn but this is not necessarily bad devolution. As much as I love reading history, its greatest disadvantage is that it requires one actually read it; critically think about its vast collection of dates, numbers, names, and other such facts; have the time and energy to gradually build up sufficient historical knowledge to imagine and critically think about the world; and then to actually imagine and critically think about the world. Instead of reading 900 pages on the French Revolution, it is much easier to read a tweet, a NY Times or other media fake story called news about it, or watch a Netflix movie about it. As John Ford said through his newspaper character in the great movie *The Man Who Shot Liberty Valance*, "[w]hen the legend becomes fact, print the legend."

However, history in death has left us an inheritance consisting of its lesson that we should not be disheartened by its death. History has only been around for about twenty-five hundred years, and its influence was limited to the literate with the desire and time to read it and use it to make history. Its life only goes back to approximately 450BC when Herodotus wrote his *The Histories* on the origins of the Greco-Persian Wars and Thucydides wrote *The History of the Peloponnesian War*. Historians consider these two to be the founders of history by their break from the Greek Homeric storytelling tradition instead to treat historical subjects by a systemic methodological method of investigation of facts and then critically writing them into a narrative. Before them and long after them well into the 20th Century for those communities lacking history, the myth and storytelling tradition was the means for transfer of knowledge and power from a past to a present found in "all corners of the world"[23]. It was during this prehistory without history that: humanity spread across the globe; created language, mathematics, astronomy, and agriculture; discovered or invented bronze, copper, and iron; survived natural disasters and human misery that modern humanity cannot even imagine; and much more was accomplished that in many ways pale the accomplishments of modern humanity lacking any

---

[23] Foley, John; E. Anne MacKay, ed. *Signs of Orality*. Brill Academic: Leiden, Netherlands (1999) pp. 1–2.

imagination to believe in the unknown because we see the known. So, one should not diminish the power of myth and storytelling. According to mythologists and other scholars studying comparative mythology and storytelling, such as the famous Joseph John Campbell and his *magnum opus* book *The Hero with a Thousand Faces,* myths and storytelling and the creation of epic poetry for easier memorization and transmission of myths and stories from community to community were passed for millennia in prehistory with equal access for all because it was an oral not written means of communication. The "power of myth" is its ability not only to give meaning to our lives but to make us appreciate "the adventure of being alive".[24]

Post modern social justice theory worships storytelling and story tellers, yet it seems to have missed completely "the adventure of being alive" concept — not only missed it but they seem to have gone the other route to promoting self-genocide for the Other.

Toni Morrison is supposedly one of the greatest living story tellers in the United States and worshiped as the epitome of African-American writing (even though she and all her family as far back as her family history is available were all born in the United States).  She claims, "I'm writing for black people … I don't have to apologize"[25]. Apologize for what? Perhaps she should apologize for the following statement she wrote during the 1998 impeachment attempts of President Clinton that reveals her true upper class opinion of the African-Americans she supposedly represents by arguing that Clinton had been mistreated because of his "Blackness":

> Years ago, in the middle of the Whitewater investigation, one heard the first murmurs: white skin notwithstanding, this is our first black President. Blacker than any actual black person who could ever be elected in our children's lifetime. After all, Clinton displays

---

[24] *The Power of Myth* video interview and dialogue between Campbell and writer/journalist Bill Moyers.
http://www.butler-bowdon.com/joseph-campbell---power-of-myth.html

[25]

https://www.theguardian.com/books/2015/apr/25/toni-morrison-books-interview-god-help-the-child

almost every trope of blackness: single-parent household, born poor, working-class, saxophone-playing, McDonald's-and-junk-food-loving boy from Arkansas.[26]

This opinion that "Blackness" is synonymous with white trash that happens to be black seems to be implicit in all her novels. I see why she is so popular with rich white folks; she confirms their opinion of what trash the poor and working class are, white or black.[27]

From various biographies of her and interviews available on the internet, we know she grew up middle class; always had support from family and friends; and lived a life of relative privilege enjoying everything the United States has to offer such as education, money, and prestige. Yet, her masterpiece story *Beloved* starts out with an outright fraudulent dedication to the "60 million" who died in the Atlantic slave trade, a number that is at least five times the number who were traded[28] and nowhere near the truth on the death rates that were higher for the crew of slave ships than for the slaves[29] — just serves as further proof that history is dead.

It then goes on to tell a story loosely based on the life of Margaret

---

[26] Morrison, Toni. (October 5, 1998). "Talk of the Town: Comment". The New Yorker.

[27] For a good history on this issue, there is Isenberg, Nancy. *White Trash.* Viking Press: N.Y., N.Y. (2016).

[28] Thomas, Hugh. *The Slave Trade, The Story of the Atlantic Slave Trade: 1440-1870.* Simon & Schuster. (February 3, 1999).

[29] "The primary aim of merchants in the late eighteen century was to minimize slave deaths in the middle passage to ensure a profitable voyage. Minimizing crew mortality was a secondary condition". Behrendt, Stephen. "Crew mortality in the transatlantic slave trade in the eighteenth century". *Slavery and Abolition,* 18:1, 49-71. DOI: 10.1080/01440399708575203

Garner, an antebellum escaped slave who killed one of her children and supposedly tried to kill the others in order to prevent them from living in slavery but was too much of a coward to kill herself. Apparently, the life of a slave instead of death was good enough for her but it was too much of a burden to give the gift of life to her children unlike all the other slave mothers throughout history. The story makes a heroine of Garner and is beloved by upper class feminists in need of rationalizing their self-centered lives focused entirely on "self-identity" in which children are seen as the property of the mother and as her "choice". Supposedly, the entire novel is about the need to develop a sense of self-identity and of the Other, though predictively the Other always winds up being someone who confirms the woman's self-identity. The Other never appears as someone who is knowingly and intentionally willing to kill their other and me as is often the reality of life.

How there can be self-identity in a world in which all identity and thus including self-identity is a social construct is a problem that Morrison leaves unexamined and the contradiction ignored — I will be examining this question later in this essay. As Wittgenstein's Private Language Argument firmly established, there is no such thing as a private language and thus no such thing as a self-identity of which we can speak existing independent of our social identity. The reality of post-modernism's own social construct theories is that we, including our self-identity, are what society says we are. I can see how Morrison's storytelling helps upper class feminists concerned with "finding themselves" in their lives of privilege but how does it help the black poor and oppressed by telling them to be self-centered?

Luckily, the stories, fiction, myths, and the reality I heard and saw while growing up with my and other working class mothers described tough women who loved their children more than themselves; who saw in their children hope for a better future regardless of their present misery; and who once their children were old enough to take care of each other then worked to earn money for the family along with their husband and the father of their children because they had to work by economic necessity not as a career choice. As silly as it now seems, it was only a couple of generations ago when storytelling required a man or a woman in order to be considered a man or a woman to be married and supporting a family. Of course, this type of storytelling had its own problems that were the exact opposites of those depicted in Morrison's tales: the working class identity was so intertwined in the family and its surrounding social identity that they create all sorts of hate, including the hate of racism, toward anyone outside or a threat to their family and social identity. These hates were not a rational matter of self-identity, oneness, or of the Other as they are for Morrison and her worshipers, but merely a means for survival in life. Never underestimate the power of hate to help one survive life threatening situations.

Throughout history (there I go again), the working class individual could not survive alone or in small groups as the rich can, they need each other. I was so indoctrinated by this community concept that I remember watching *Sophie's Choice* and being disgusted by its heroine who allowed a Nazi to force a choice between which of her children would live, and then who after their deaths eventually goes on to live in the United States. I could not imagine a tough working class woman being such a traitor to her family as to allow a Nazi to force such a choice upon her and then live herself. I started imagining such women only upon meeting the women of Harvard Law School. Sophie was at best someone to be pitied not to be understood. The Nazi sure had an understanding of what she would do and used this understanding to destroy her spiritually and her family both spiritually and physically. The goal of good storytelling is to defeat that understanding and its power not to confirm it.

This was the tough mythology I learned and that represents the "power of myth" for poor black or white trash in my youth. Ultimately, as the song goes, "united we'll fail, divided we'll fall"[30], but at least through the millennia such myths allowed plebeians to put up a fight. As misguided as they appear now, at least they gave me and others the will, the hope, and the support for the proverbial Fight the Powers. There was no concern for self-identity, a selfish concern not present in good working class storytelling — except as an evil — because it was not and is not a luxury they can afford. As bad as this old school story telling might have been from a moral perspective and the societal hate it ultimately promoted, I fail to see how the story telling of a Toni Morrison promoting self-identity and the selfish concentration on oneness and on a delusional Other that reinforce that selfishness as the ultimate good are any better, especially when by her own admission the social identity as seen from the Others on high — such as from her — of both the white and black poor and working class is that of social trash.

Other popular social justice storytellers such a James Baldwin and Ta-Nehisi Coates are even worse storytellers. Unlike Morrison whose self-genocide storytelling does not affect her or her feminist readers by only the Other and their children and the family that they see only as property or as a choice, Black writers such as Baldwin and Coates are promoting self-

---

[30] Antivist, *Bring Me the Horizon.*

genocide upon themselves as men by their stories, but they are either too dense or too selfish to acknowledge it. Being a history nerd for another moment, according to the Tuskegee Institute and FBI crime statistics "[t]here were approximately 2,936 black-on-black homicides in six months of 2012 and 3,446 black lynchings from 1882-1896."[31] Thus more blacks murder blacks each year than the so-called genocide by lynching that whiteness murdered in more than a hundred years? What is the storytelling response to such historical tragedy by story tellers Baldwin and Coates?

According to various biographies, Baldwin was recognized as a writing talent by age nine and received mentorship and help including the publishing of his first story by age thirteen from numerous teachers and influential adults, both white and black. So much so that by 1948 at the age of 24 he made a good enough income as a writer to expatriate to France and live there the rest of his life freely and openly as he wished to live as a gay black man. So what did he do from France the rest of his life? He spent it complaining about the United States while not mentioning it was the United States and its Allies that freed France from the Nazis allowing him to live there as he wished. Three years earlier, when the world was fighting to free countries such as France from Nazism so that Baldwin could later live there, he was working in a nice war factory job in New Jersey. While in New Jersey, according to his *Notes of a Native Son*, one day he became very angry by the many restaurants that would not serve him as a black man. So, what did he do? Fight the Powers and take on the racist white men, restaurant owners, managers, state, police, or the Man? No, he picked up a mug and threw it at the working class waitress doing her job and then ran away thus pretty much confirming the low opinion perpetuated of black men by racists. Based on the working class storytelling I heard as a child, Baldwin was a coward who beat up on women and then ran away including to another country — but only after the misery of others had made the other country

---

[31] http://archive.tuskegee.edu/archive/bitstream/handle /123456789/511/Lyching%201882%201968.pdf?se quence=1&isAllowed=y; https://ucr.fbi.gov/crime-in-the-u.s/2012/crime-in-th e-u.s.-2012/offenses-known-to-law-enforcement/ex panded-homicide/expanded_homicide_data_table_6 _murder_race_and_sex_of_vicitm_by_race_and_se x_of_offender_2012.xls

safe for him. According to post-modern social justice story telling, Baldwin is a heroic Black? As the Black working class hero Thomas Sowell wrote:

> Celebrated black writer James Baldwin, for example, claimed that blacks took the building of a subsidized housing project in Harlem as "additional proof of how thoroughly the white world despised them" because "people in Harlem know they are living there because white people do not think they are good enough to live anywhere else."  Therefore "they had scarcely moved in" to the new housing project, before "naturally they began smashing windows, defacing walls, urinating in the elevators and fornicating in the playgrounds."
>
> From this perspective, anything negative that blacks do is the fault of whites.  But however much Baldwin's picture might fit the prevailing vision of the 1960s, anyone who is serious about whether it also fits the facts would have to ask such questions as: (1) Was there a time before the 1960s when it was common for blacks to urinate in public areas of buildings where they lived? and (2) If not, was that because they felt that whites had higher regard for them in earlier times?
>
> To ask such questions is to answer them, and the answer in both cases is clearly *No!** But few asked such questions, which remained outside the sealed bubble of the prevailing vision. What was different about the 1960s was the proliferation of people like James Baldwin, promoting resentments and polarization, and making excuses for counter-productive and even barbaric behavior. Nor is this phenomena peculiar to blacks or even to the United States. Writing about lower class whites in British public housing projects, Dr. Theodore Dalrymphle observed:  "The public spaces and elevators of all public housing blocks I know are so deeply impregnated with urine that the color is ineradicable and anything smashable has been smashed."
>
> *As a personal note, I lived in Harlem in the 1940s and 1950s, when no one expected the smell of urine to be normal in places where blacks lived. Others familiar with that period likewise paint a radically different picture of the projects of that area. For example: "These were not the projects of idle, stinky elevators, of gant controlled stairwells where drug dealers go down. In the 1940's, 50's and 60's, when most of the city's public housing was built, a sense of pride and community permeated well-kept corridors,

apartments and grounds." Lizette Alvarez, "Out and Up," *New York Times*, May 31, 2009, Metropolitan section, page 1. The projects in which economist Walter Williams grew up in Philadelphia in that era were likewise radically different from the projects of later years. Walter E. Williams, *Up From the Projects: An Autobiography* (Stanford: Hoover Institution Press, 2010) pages 4 to 8.  There was certainly not less discrimination and racism in the earlier period so the difference was not due to white people.  Among the differences between the two eras was that the intelligentsia, both black and white, became more prone in the latter period to make excuses such as James Baldwin made for moral squalor and barbaric behavior. After such notions permeated the society, barbaric behavior and moral squalor became accepted norms within some segments of society – and among many intellectuals observing those segments of society.[32]

Transforming the art and power of story-telling into the art of telling rich people what they want to hear about Blackness and into self-genocide has been perfected by Ta-Nehisi Coates, the so-called new James Baldwin. According to his books about his life and various interviews and internet biographies of him, from the perspective of an average person, Coates comes from a highly educated, prosperous, comfortable, and even prestigious family. His parents (plus at least one if not all of his grandparents), siblings, and close relatives were college educated. His mother was a teacher. His father not only published and wrote books but eventually became a university librarian at Howard University. Coates had the good fortune to receive every opportunity the United States and life in general have to give an individual: well-educated parents who taught him reading and writing beginning at age three; excellent schooling such as French classes in grade seven; attendance at the nationally acclaimed Baltimore Polytechnic High School; an extended family with plenty of financial and emotional support; older siblings who all became successful college educated professionals and thus plenty of good role models; a free ride to Howard University; the only violence inflicted upon him instead of by him upon others was by his dad; and he never had any experience with police or crime other than causing it and getting away with it such as battering two of his high school teachers.

---

[32] Sowell, T. *Intellectuals and Race.* pp. 90-91.

What does he do with all this opportunity? He barely graduates high school despite avoiding jail after physically assaulting two teachers; was a bully in grade school and high school not only to his teachers but to his supposed brother "black bodies"; and complains of being forced to take "seventh grade French". "Seventh grade French"! In my neighborhood, until maybe high school if you did not drop out, the only foreign language experience we received was the language you spoke at home after finishing your classes in English in school. After graduating from high school, he went on to college for five years but he failed to graduate. Apparently this genius was the first in his family not to graduate from college — though he wasted five years, a lot of his family's money, and Howard University's financial assistance that could have gone to someone who really wanted and needed it trying to complete what has become a relatively simple task if you can afford the tuition. He has never had a real job in his whole life other than writing about what white people should be doing and excusing his wasted opportunities in life. Despite his failure to graduate, he is well versed enough in the workings of academia to attend some type of graduate program in French at Middlebury College so that he can attend a "fellowship" in Paris to admire how wide French doors are, sit in cafes, and walk the streets of Paris, laughing from afar at the American *bourgeoisie* and *hoi polloi* and thus following the worst traditions of the French intelligentsia and his predecessor James Baldwin. While doing so, he apparently was and is completely ignorant of the fact that he was only able to do so because many of those *bourgeoisie* and *hoi polloi* died to free Paris from the Nazis, the last major Western proponents of slavery and racism, while that same intelligentsia were doing the same then as they do now: sitting in cafes, walking Paris, and laughing at Americans only at that time they did it with the Nazis instead of with Coates.

Coates is educated enough to know that "[f]ully 60 percent of all young black men who drop out of high school will go to jail." As society gets more complex and even the simplest of tasks require more education, this statistic will likely worsen. Even the conservative, narrow American formal education that he has completed has given Coates money and power and he should be nothing by grateful to the educational system that has given them to him. Instead, knowing what he does about what happens to dropouts, what does he do? He ridicules it. Mr. Coates thinks school is "only an opportunity to discipline the body", that involves "writing between the lines", "copying the directions legibly", and "memorizing theorems". He writes "[t]hey were concerned with compliance" and "Algebra, Biology, English" are just excuses for "discipline." What a miserable person he is. If Mr. Coates thinks schools are boring, authoritarian, uncaring, and only concerned that students follow orders and generate a profit for the school, then Mr. Coates should try work, the type of work that he has apparently spent a lifetime either avoiding or failing to accomplish but that provides the bread and butter for the vast majority of the rest of the world, both the working and middle classes. Work in which you are expected to show up on time, spend your day at whatever tedious task your employer orders you to do that day, wait until you are allowed to leave, go home, and then come back the next day to repeat the cycle again. He has no more experience with wage slavery than he does with chattel slavery.

He is now a "genius" because he writes what rich white people want to hear about Blacks. Slavery and being black is the best thing that ever happened to him or he would be just another college drop out white dude with no future and no past that anyone cared about. His storytelling is worse than any storytelling by racists ridiculing blackness because at least those stories gave black youth something to fight against, Coates only glorifies cowardice.

I read better story telling in the comic books of my youth. This is why I saw some flame of hope in the recent popularity of the comic Black Panther but of course it was quickly blown out by associating it with "Blackness". The name "Black Panther" is associated with blackness historically through the Black Panther Party that I saw rise in the Chicagoland area. It was one of many street gangs that took advantage of the chaos of the Sixties to made money introducing drugs and guns into black neighborhoods in addition to pimping out their women. Of course, as is common with criminal gangs, they stuck to terrorizing their own because there was too much risk coming to neighborhoods such as mine in which our own criminals and mobsters would put up too much of a fight. Coates' father supposedly was a Black Panther and fathered seven children with four or five different women. Associating the Black Panther with Blackness and the Black Panther Party is analogous to associating Captain America with being American through the American mafia — another example of self genocide story telling. The story telling I heard in my youth associated being a gang member, mobster, and criminal with being a loser. We did not glorify a Malcolm X for being a gangster eventually killed by his own for cheating with their women simply because he was charismatic as a speaker of propaganda. Our storytelling treated such failures as failures; our storytelling heros were winners because we were surrounded by losers such as Malcolm X who were to be pitied not glorified.

<u>**B.**</u>        <u>**Propaganda**</u>

History has left the building.  Storytelling. stories, and myth are back in. Not a problem for workers because we are better at story telling than any social justice warrior. The departure of history does not mean the end of history. I say this despite not even having discussed workers' greatest storytelling: Christianity and Jesus Christ, both hero and antihero.

The big question is whether storytelling has become propaganda? Stories and story telling are passed among physical individuals and communities including within social classes and are thus within their control to be changed as necessary to fit their needs and to give them a sense of power and hope in the physical reality of life. Propaganda serves "to create an abstract universe, representing a complete reconstruction of reality in the minds of its citizens"[33]. Before we get into this issue, I need to contemplate the concept of "social construct" and do a bit more contemplation of that aspect of the death of history in which those with normative power have the power to negate or to enforce what history "ought to be" in any given situation.

---

[33] Ellul, J. *The Technological Society*. p. 371.

<u>**C.**</u>　　　　<u>**History and "the problem of the color-line"**</u>

The book *"Color Conscious: The Political Morality of Race"* begins with an Introduction by David Wilkins in which the first line is: "In 1903, W.E.B. Du Bois proclaimed that 'the problem of the twentieth century is the problem of the color-line.'"[34] The second line is: "As we approach the end of the millennium, the accuracy of Du Bois's prophecy is beyond dispute".[35] It is fitting that Professor Wilkins is a professor at my alma mater Harvard Law School because these two lines say so much about the power held by the intellectual proletariat that operate upper class and ruling class institutions such as Harvard. Even when they have no clue as to what they are talking about, it still sounds more intelligent and has more power than anything said by anyone that has a clue. The historical significance of Du Bois' prophecy is that it is both nonsense and yet undisputedly true by Harvard's class power to make prophecies come true.

"The problem of the twentieth century is the problem of the color-line". Really? So, five hundred or a thousand years from now when any historians that remain look back at the 20th Century and see two World Wars; the final death thralls of at least four and possibly five world empires[36]; the

------

[34] Appiah, Kwame A.; Gutmann, Amy. *Color Conscious: The Political Morality of Race.* Princeton University Press: Princeton, New Jersey (March 16, 1998). p. 3.

[35] *Ibid*

[36] British, German, Austria-Hungarian, Ottoman, and possibly even the Roman. In my readings, I came across this interesting history story (This is why I still love history):

> Peter Charanis, born on the island in 1908 and later a professor of Byzantine history at Rutgers University recounts when the island was occupied and Greek soldiers were sent to the villages and stationed themselves in the public squares. Some of the children ran

United States transforming from a fairly insignificant regional power with an antiquated military to the most powerful economic empire in history; the rise and fall of communism and the start and ending of the Cold War which by themselves involved the murder and genocide deaths of hundreds of millions; and then there is the birth of the Nuclear Age, the Age of Science, the Space Age, and the Technological Society that for example eliminated small pox from the earth for the first time in world history and allowed a healthy long-living world population to rise from one billion to six billion in a just Century; all of this will be ignored to see "the color-line" as "the problem" of the Century? How can anyone let alone a tenured professor at supposedly one of the top universities in the world make such a stupid statement?

What color-line? What do they mean by "color-line"? Maybe the "color-line" is a synonym for "race" and "racism" thus it refers to the race problem in Europe between the intelligentsia fabricated race of "Aryan" and its struggle to resolve its intelligentsia-created problem with "the Jew" that resulted in the largest European genocide of the 20th Century? Or, perhaps he is referring to Asia in which race hatred between various Chinese, Korean, and Japanese ethnicities that go back centuries resulted in ten years of war, tens of millions of deaths, and such infamous battles as the Rape of Nanking and the Japanese Stalingard of New Guinea?

Of course not, it must mean the color line separating Du Bois and Wilkins as black from those who are white. And what will historians study about this 20th Century "problem of the color-line"? How the power of the British Empire and other Western Powers in less than a century for the first

---

to see what Greek soldiers looked like. ''What are you looking at?'' one of them asked. ''At Hellenes,'' the children replied. ''Are you not Hellenes yourselves?'' a soldier retorted. ''No, we are Romans''. Thus was the most ancient national identity in all of history, preserved in isolation, finally absorbed and ended. Kaldellis, A. (2008). *Hellenism in Byzantium: The Transformations of Greek Identity and the Reception of the Classical Tradition.* Cambridge, UK: Cambridge University Press. ISBN 0521876885. pages 42-43

time in world history by the 20<sup>th</sup> Century forcibly ended chattel slavery throughout Western Civilization regardless of the color of the slaves? How Western Civilization in the 20<sup>th</sup> Century successfully and forcibly ended chattel slavery in Africa among its many tribes made up of hundreds of different ethnicities and nationalities that are treated by this prophecy as simply a color and also ended it in Eastern Civilization regardless of color so that for the first time in world history chattel slavery was wiped from the Earth? Perhaps they will study how the approximate 600,000 slaves transported to the United States before the slave trade was abolished in 1808 became 4,000,000 by the 1860's, and 40,000,000 self-described as "black" on the national census just a century-and-a-half later[37]?  No, none of this is "the problem". In fact, simply by making some such suggestions, many consider me the problem as a white man ridiculing a prophecy made by a great black man so obviously I must be a racist. Any history I give is worthless to protecting me from such accusations because history is dead.

One of the major problems of the 20<sup>th</sup> and of any Century begins with the individual myopic self-centered view of the world, of themselves, and of history that is shared by all humans regardless of "color-line". This perspective problem if I am allowed to be a history nerd for a few moments more is the most powerful and has the most significant effect on history when it is the view of a Century's most powerful nation and its Powers such as those of the United States. For any human individual, more often than not, their problems seem to them to be the world's problems or should be. There is nothing wrong with this view. "Life, Liberty and the pursuit of Happiness" in the United States Declaration of Independence are supposedly "self-evident" examples of  "unalienable rights" the Declaration says have been "endowed by their Creator" upon humanity and for which governments are created to protect. Everyone only has one life to live and they might as well try to live it their way. Regardless of how normatively humans ought to be, empirically, one can do all the scientific experimentation possible on one's or anyone's visual field in all possible worlds viewed but in none of them will one ever find the inner limit or the point from which its contents are seen because the existential observer or individual consciousness is it; without the consciousness of the observer there is no visual field. No one ought to be anything other than the center of their world.

However, as an emigrant to the United States who loves it and spent six years of my life dedicated to its defense including spending more than

---

[37] http://blackdemographics.com/population/

two of those years underwater in its defense and would do so again if the need arises, the people of the United States regardless of their "colorline" need to get over this myopic delusion that your problems are the Century's problems. Though I believe and agree with native-born patriots that the United States is a great country and most likely the greatest in history so far, but unfortunately most of this greatness is built on potential and hope. The United States is truly the hope of the world but you have not as yet lived up to your potential and there is no guarantee that you ever will. You have been blessed by the Fates: 1) with existing East/West between two oceans shielding you from the rest of the world; 2) with friendly or at least nonthreatening neighbors to you North and South; 3) with never knowing massive invasions and its ravages on your land except for the American Civil War that in comparison to the multiple civil wars[38] suffered by most of the rest of the world was fairly average as civil wars go[39]; and 4) blessed with never knowing millennia of struggle including genocide and resulting entrenched hate among competing tribes that is in the heart and soul of the rest of the World. My homeland of tiny little Croatia has more than 50 wars

---

[38] The Roman Republic had 13 civil wars just in its last 150 years before it became the Roman Principate or Empire as we know it. https://en.wikipedia.org/wiki/Roman_civil_wars.

[39] The United States suffered approximately 620,000 casualties in its Civil War or 2% of its population that was about 10% of its Northern military age population and about 20% of its Southern male population. https://www.civilwar.org/learn/articles/civil-war-fac ts; https://blogs.ancestry.com/cm/12-stunning-civil-wa r-facts/. Just in the Taiping Rebellion fought at roughly the same time, China lost 20 million at the low end of the estimates or 10% of its population. http://www.newworldencyclopedia.org/entry/Taipin g_Rebellion

listed in its Wikipedia page[40] with its last civil war occurring <25 years ago. It would take a book just to list the wars fought on the ground of my other homeland Italy. One of the few facts I know of the males in my Istrian family background is as follows: 1) my great-grandfather was conscripted by the Austro-Hungarian Empire to fight the Italians; 2) my grandfather was conscripted by the Italians to fight the Austro-Hungarian Empire; 3) my father was conscripted by Yugoslavia to fight both the remnants of the Empire and Italy; 4) I enlisted in the United States Navy to fight the world. One civil war, that's it; and it is all you whine about? You really need to get over it.

Genocide? For four years between 1945 and 1949, the United States was the only country in the world with atomic weapons. If you wanted to commit genocide and conquer the world, you had plenty of opportunity to do so. Everyone in the United States throws this word "genocide" around but except for the few Holocaust survivors remaining, none really know what it means. What about the so-called Native Americans such as the warrior, slave owning, human sacrificing theocracies of the Aztecs, Incas, and so forth? As historians continuously repeat and everyone ignores because history is dead, 90% - 95% of so-called Native America populations were killed off by Mother Nature through its diseases such as small pox, measles, and even the flu. Those diseases killed many more in the Old World than in the New World; just as malaria and even the Tsetse Fly and the diseases it spread were "enormously powerful all[ies] of the Africans in resisting European incursions"[41].

Real genocide consists of knowingly and intentionally wiping out an entire community, tribe, race, group, population of people, or whatever you want to call the enemy target of genocide. The only example even remotely known to Americans is the Holocaust that Americans fought to stop not to accomplish. Even the genocide of one million Cambodians by the Khmer Rouge after we lost the Vietnam War is forgotten. My best example of the true nature of genocide is that by the Athenian Empire committed on the population of Melos they cold-bloodedly justified with the following honest

---

[40]

https://en.wikipedia.org/wiki/List_of_wars_involvin g_Croatia

[41] Sowell, T. *Conquests and Cultures*. Basic Books: N.Y., N.Y. (1998) p. 114.

realist view of politics:

> For ourselves, we shall not trouble you with specious pretenses -
> either of how we have a right to our empire because we overthrew
> the Mede, or are now attacking you because of wrong that you have
> done us - and make a long speech which would not be believed; and
> in return we hope that you, instead of thinking to influence us by
> saying that you did not join the Lacedaemonians, although their
> colonists, or that you have done us no wrong, will aim at what is
> feasible, holding in view the real sentiments of us both; since you
> know as well as we do that right, as the world goes, is only in
> question between equals in power, while the strong do what they can
> and the weak suffer what they must.[42]

Regardless, ignoring history as we must, Du Bois' prophecy has undisputedly come true. Here we are a few years after having elected twice a President Obama who according to Du Bois and Wilkins is on the wrong side of the "color-line"; when for the first time in human history we have the power to eliminate poverty, hunger, and illiteracy from the world; and when there is an entire universe out there waiting to be discovered, explored, and conquered; so what are we spending time and energy doing? I am and a significant part of the efforts of academia, government, and private industry are wasting considerable resources that could be much better spend elsewhere arguing about race and racism and the "color-line". What gives?

Such waste is occurring despite the fact there were other opinions made at the time and soon after Du Bois made his prophecy that looked much more promising for eliminating a "color-line" problem. The Black-American writer George S. Schulyer in 1926 wrote *The Negro Art Hokum*[43] denying there was such a thing as "black art" or a black sensibility, and that black artists in the United States were and should be treated as equally diverse as white artists. He argues that to expect a uniform style or subject

---

[42] Thucydides. *History of the Peloponnesian War.* Chapter XVII "Sixteenth Year of the War - The Melian Conference - Fate of Melos" (431 B.C.).
https://www.mtholyoke.edu/acad/intrel/melian.htm

[43] http://historymatters.gmu.edu/d/5129/

matter as being "Blackness" was as insulting as the stereotypes that were being rejected. He went on to write the novel *Black No More* ridiculing both racists and those who pretended to be non-racist by satirizing them to be essentially of the same kind. Unfortunately, as a result of his opposition to almost all mainstream black leaders from W.E.B. Du Bois to Martin Luther King as is true of Thomas Sowell in present day, he became an outcaste and estranged from popular black writers and now must be rediscovered to be appreciated. It was his opponents with their prophecies of a mandatory color-line that became mainstream and still are; such as Langston Hughes arguing that black artists painting anything but images of African Americans was wanting to be white[44], and James Weldon Johnson ending his fictional story *The Autobiography of An Ex-Colored Man:* "I cannot repress the thought, that, after all, I have chosen the lesser part, that I have sold my birthright for a mess of pottage".[45]

What gives? How did such a relatively minor problem as a "color-line" in the mess that is the modern world that should have disappeared at the latest with the election of a black President become not only a problem but "the problem" for the United States that its intelligentsia is now trying to export to other countries[46]? Again, we must forget history, it is worthless in

---

[44]  http://historymatters.gmu.edu/d/5129/

[45] Johnson, James W. *The Autobiography of An Ex-Colored Man.* Sherman, French & Co.: Boston, MA. (1912) p. 207.

[46] Nobles, Melissa. *Shades of citizenship: Race and the Census in Modern Politics.* Stanford: Stanford University Press (2000). This book deals with Professor Noble of MIT after finding racism in the US Census then going to Brazil to tell it that it has a race problem it does not know about despite a few hundred years of inter-marriage and intermixing. Exporting Blackness and racism to Brazil, the great intelligentsia contribution to the US export economy.

contemplating such a question. I will go on now to contemplate a conceptual analysis of the nature of social construct and ontology.

# III.    IS A "SOCIAL CONSTRUCT" A SOCIAL CONSTRUCT OR AN ONTOLOGY?

*When I think in words, I don't have 'meanings' in my mind in addition to the verbal expressions, language itself is the vehicle of thought.* — Ludwig Wittgenstein

The words "social construct" are thrown around so much these days as a means to ridicule any claims of knowledge or truth that these words have become so ambiguous as to be almost meaningless as anything more than polemics. To paraphrase Humpty-Dumpty:

"I don't know what you mean by '[social construct],' " Alice said. Humpty Dumpty smiled contemptuously. "Of course you don't — till I tell you. I meant 'there's a nice knock-down argument for you!' "
"But [social construct] doesn't mean 'a nice knock-down argument'," Alice objected.
"When I use a word," Humpty Dumpty said, in rather a scornful tone, "it means just what I choose it to mean—neither more nor less."
"The question is," said Alice, "whether you can make words mean so many different things."
"The question is," said Humpty Dumpty, "which is to be master—that's all."[47]

Relative to my contemplation of race and class, I need to know who is the master: the words or the speaker. Language in all its forms varies from words and numbers to purely visual means of communications and everything in between. We cannot think logically or illogically without using some form of language. Without language, we simply have action or nonsense. 'Nonsense' consists of undefinable words or images that cannot state a logical possibility; but, I must have language in order even to define or communicate with you what is nonsense. However, the power of language goes beyond the

---

[47] Lewis Carroll's *Through the Looking-Glass.* McMillan & Co.: London. (1872) p. 124

power of logic and is, perhaps unfortunately, not limited to matters of which we can speak because such a limitation would prevent us speaking about some of the most important questions in life. "We feel that even if all possible scientific questions be answered, the problems of life have still not been touched at all."[48] Even nonsense language is not totally without use or useless because it can have aesthetic meaning such as exemplified by the logician and mathematician Lewis Carroll's *Jabberwocky*. Really, the only completely meaningless language would be a cacophony of noise.

The philosophical contemplation of language in its earliest forms goes back to Plato, Aristotle, and the Roman Stoic schools of philosophy. However, it took up a dominant role in philosophy in the 20th Century when science took up a dominant role in Western Civilization. The language of science with its scientific methodology using mathematics as its language became the fashionable language to be, including for philosophy. Problem is, how do we do it? How do we make all language scientific language? In making this attempt, there developed a collection of philosophies commonly known as logical positivism and early analytic philosophy. This analytic school of philosophy argued the sole purpose of philosophy is to help science and other scientific disciplines dealing with sense experience problems to maintain clear and logical syntax and semantics for their theories and solutions. The logical positivist goal was normative: to develop a language by which science ought to describe reality through logic and words verifiable or defined by sense experience. Regarding purely philosophical inquiries such as metaphysics, ontology, morality, philosophy of mind, epistemology, theology, aesthetics, and politics, these simply express confusion over the syntax and semantics of words and language; certain subjects of human consciousness simply cannot be talked about. Thus comes the famous expression, "[w]hereof one cannot speak, thereof one must be silent".[49]

Normally, historically, when philosophy finds an answer to a

---

[48] Wittgenstein, Ludwig. *Philosophical Investigations,* translation from the German by G.E.M. Anscombe, at Proposition 6.52. Wiley-Blackwell, 4th edition (2009).

[49] Wittgenstein, Ludwig. *Tractatus Logico-Philosophicus,* translation from the German by C. K. Ogden, at Proposition 7. Dover Publications, 471st edition (1998).

question it is contemplating, it becomes a science. Physics, chemistry, biology and such were all once branches of philosophy, until they started getting answers that worked. Unfortunately, this has not happened in logic nor in the analytic philosophy of language and science; there seems to be no likelihood of it happening in the near future despite pretensions by such wordgames as linguistic mentalism. This failure occurred because the language of all sense experience is laden with the language of ideas and theory. The unfortunate epistemological reality is that sense perception is unavoidably intertwined with theory expressed by language that is itself laden with theory. Thus language often decides what facts we experience, observe, and use. As Albert Einstein said, "whether you can observe a thing or not depends on the theory which you use. It is the theory which decides what can be observed".[50] Better yet is the description by Ludwig Wittgenstein: "the limits of my language mean the limits of my world."[51] Though they did not doubt the ontological existence of a reality beyond language, speaking about it was a problem.

Thus, because all language by necessity will contain doubt, modern Western analytic philosophy has — at least for now — given up on logical positivism as well as on the foundationalism of Plato or Descartes seeking to know truth directly and to define knowledge descriptively through the language of ideas and logical theory that cannot be doubted. It has also — at least for now — given up on any empiricism seeking to define knowledge based solely on the language of sense experience or of logical constructs based on sense experience because the language of all sense experience is laden with the language of ideas and theory and thus of epistemic vagueness, uncertainty, and doubt. Epistemology is still struggling to define knowledge, belief, and truth and skepticism as to whether any such defining is possible.

Meanwhile, at the other end of the spectrum going away from analytic philosophy and toward the studies commonly known as continental philosophy, those schools of thought jumped on the failure of logical positivism, on the epistemic inability to define what if anything we know there exists outside of our sensations, on the necessary indeterminacy and

---

[50] Salam, A.; H. A. Bethe; P. Dirac; W. Heisenberg; E. P. Wigner; O. Klein, E. M. Lifshitz. *From a Life of Physics.* p. 40. Singapore, World Scientific (1989).

[51] *Tractatus Logico-Philosophicus* at 5.6.

vagueness of language, and on Wittgenstein's "[t]he meaning of a word is its use"[52] first to argue phenomenalism and then to argue reality to be a social construct of the uses and usefulness of language. Thus for these philosophers and their progeny, the meaning of a word was not logic nor some metaphysical "thing-in-itself" existing independently of our sensations or of other words, but its use and usefulness in life's physical and social interactions. This argument eventually led to the concept of deconstruction of language as a means to understand sense experience reality solely based on the deconstruction of the empirical reality of words, sentences, and their structure. Adding a Nietzschean world view, all language is used and is useful as a means for power — except, as far as I can tell, for those doing the deconstruction.

As far as modern philosophy goes, "[w]hat we got here is a failure to communicate."[53] Getting caught up in these metaphysical debates on the ultimate nature of reality will not help me on contemplating race and class. Need to be more practical.

---

[52] Wittgenstein, Ludwig. *Philosophical Investigations,* at Proposition 43.

[53] Newman, Paul. As character Luke in film *Cool Hand Luke* (1967).

<u>A.</u>      <u>What are social constructs and what is ontologically a fact?</u>

Attempting to make sense of this mess, in a series of articles and books by such philosophers as Ian Hacking in the philosophy of science and Alvin Goldman in epistemology, philosophy has been able to identify and describe a spectrum of meanings for "social construct" varying from a weak version to a strong version.[54] The weak version claims that any language, including scientific language, about any reality that exists independent of us is at least in part determined by human interest and goals and as such are socially constructed and not inevitable attributes of that independent reality. The strong version makes the more dramatic argument that we know no reality independent of properties and facts socially constructed by language and thus reality itself is a social construct that does not exist independent of our language for it.

As if social construction and its various versions were not controversial enough, Hacking and other philosophers[55] further point out that there is almost always implied a normative aspect wherein when referring to something as a social construct it is meant it is harmful. So, for example, the common postmodern social justice argument regarding gender defined as female and male is not only that it is not caused by biology but instead by social processes, the argument goes further to argue it is harmful by making the male gender dominate over the female gender and thus normatively ought to be revised or eliminated. Their solution is a transgender, multi-gender,

---

[54] Goldman, Alvin. *Knowledge in a Social World.* Oxford University Press (1999); Goldman, Alvin. "What is Social Epistemology? A Smorgasbord of Projects". *Pathways to Knowledge, Private and Public.* Oxford University Press (2002) pp. 182-204; Hacking, Ian. *The Social Construction of What?* Harvard University Press (1999).

[55] Hacking, Ian. *The Social Construction of What*; Boghossian, Paul. *Fear of Knowledge: Against Relativism and Constructivism*, Oxford University Press (2006) ISBN 0-19-928718-X.

queer gender, and other options creating a wide range of possibilities for gender they argue is not dependent on social construction but, as usual, on self identity thus making all genders equal — thus supposedly assuring equality of the sexes and genders. If the social construct concept were handled consistently, these alternative gender possibilities would be seen as social constructs based on human interest and goals as the two-gender option and thus accepting either, any, or all should be just a pragmatic option of which works best for the society constructing them and not an ultimate question of morality. That is, the words "social construct" should also be a social construct. However, because of the normative aspect of social construction, no post-modern social justice theory would make such an admission. Thus for them, for example again, the male/female gender option is a necessarily true evil social kind or social construct, while their solution is the necessarily true good natural kind. Unavoidably, whenever there is argument over whether something is a social construct or an ontological reality, these arguments will almost always also involve normative arguments of what ought to be that are used to decide the issue.

Clearly, some words seem to be human creations dependent on language alone that would not exist independently of language and thus are social constructs: money, property, citizenship, bravery, political offices, baseball, and so forth. Other words seem to be used to mean empirical facts existing independently of language: mountains, rivers, haystacks, rocks, thirst, hunger, fear, rage, and so forth. Seems simple enough.

Seems simple enough until you try to use these always vague and often indeterminate words as premises in your reasoning. If you are thirsty, hungry, and fearful of dying from exposure but have no money to buy food, water, or shelter, is the lack of the social kind money any less real and its effects any less deadly than the natural kinds hunger, thirst, and fear? If you have natural kind shelter and work in the United States but lack the social kind citizenship and live in the social kind status of being an illegal, is your social kind citizenship status any less of a deadly risk to your quality of life than the so-called natural kinds? How does the lack of citizenship affect your behavior and the social or the so-called self-identity of your physical self? As the ancient Sorites Paradox still unresolved by philosophy continues to point out, surely a mountain, a river, and a haystack are natural kinds independent of our language but when does a mountain become a hill, a river a stream, and a haystack just a pile of straw or the converse? Unfortunately, the unavoidable conclusion is they change from one ontological real entity to another only when social construction decides they change so.

Such paradoxes of vagueness blurring the distinction between social kinds and natural kinds are omnipresent in our language and the reality it describes. For example, everyone knows or should know a whale is a mammal not a fish; to say otherwise is to be uneducated. However, from Genesis to Melville's *Moby Dick*, a whale was a fish for the obvious reason that it lived in water. It was a fish until the mid-18th Century when the emerging science of taxonomy decided to classify animals by categories such as *Mammalia* based on attributes internal to the animal instead of external attributes such as the environment in which it lives. Thus, a whale stopped being a fish and became a mammal. This classification along with the entire hierarchy of biological classification with its eight major taxonomic ranks from "life" down to "species" with each having intermediate rankings is clearly a social construction; it would be a simple argument to make that there were no mammals nor any other taxonomic hierarchies in reality until the language of taxonomy created them. So why is anyone who says a whale is a fish considered uneducated and ignorant at best and viewed as stupid if they continue to say so? It would be a simple argument to make that taxonomy got it wrong; that is, one can make an intelligent argument it would be a better classification if a whale were classified as a fish along with everything else that lives in the water.

All words in some way are vague and blur any attempt to create a sharp divide between language and the reality language describes, so much so that some philosophers argue reality itself is vague or made up of vague objects[56]; however, some words can be used to clarify a difference between social constructs and the reality which they try to describe. For example, almost all educated persons are now familiar with the formula $E=mc^2$ with $c$ being the speed of light that is about $3\times10^{\wedge}8$ m/s and describes a constant in human observation of the universe consisting of the maximum speed of conventional massless particles and thus of information. How is it that we observe in the universe a speed limit stated in meters per second when *"metre"* as a length was not arbitrarily defined by science until 1793 and

---

[56] Rosen, Gideon; Smith, Nicholas J. J. "Worldly Indeterminacy: A Rough Guide". *Australasian Journal of Philosophy*. Vol. 82, No.1, pp. 185-198; March 2004. *Contra*: Evans, Gareth. "Can There be Vague Objects." *Analysis*, Volume 38, Issue 4, 1 October 1978, https://doi.org/10.1093/analys/38.4.208

redefined a few times afterward simply by agreement (including its most recent arbitrarily revision by agreement equaling it to a certain distance traveled by the speed of light)? Well, actually it does not. This observed speed limit defined in meters instead of any other of the infinite possibilities for its measurement is a social construct created by agreement and thus dependent on the personalities, history, and culture of those agreeing, but the *c* is not; this "*c*" represents a real constant in our human observation of the universe that could be defined as 1 or whatever number we wanted as long as we all agreed and we must agree to use the same definition everywhere there are humans observing nature regardless of the personalities, history, and culture of those observing. Regardless of how we define our measurement of it, the *c* is real and is not dependent on the personality, sex, race, class, or culture of the human observing it though its units of measurement are so dependent. The instrumentalist nature of science does not mean science is a relativistic or arbitrary social construct:

> Why is a Euclidean point just the intersection of two one-dimensional lines?  Why does a body free of impressed forces move in a straight line?  Why does Mars describe an elliptical orbit?  Why does the force of gravity vary inversely with the square of the distance?  Why does nothing move faster than light?  Why are all electrons identical?  Because the world as we now know it becomes intelligible by supposing these things to be the case.  What better reason for saying that they are the case?
>
> ...
>
> ... phenomena can be appreciated only against a conceptual pattern ...
>
> This does not mean that the principle is an empty tautology, a definition, or an arbitrary notational convention. Had nature been other than it is, or had we come to conceive of it differently, the principle never might have been formulated at all. Our nineteenth-century professor did not himself distribute the spheres in the odd way we noted; nature was supposed to do that. What he did was to harness the only conceptions which could then describe what nature had done.[57]

---

[57] Hanson, Norwood Russell. *Patterns of Discovery*. Cambridge University Press: Cambridge, UK. Re-issue (2010). pp. 134-136.

Further:

> So too the fact that it [the world] can be described by Newtonian mechanics asserts nothing about the world; but *this* asserts something, namely, that it can be described in what does tell us something about it, namely, that it can be described in that particular way in which as a matter it is described. The fact, too, that it can be described more simply by one system of mechanics than by another says something about the world.[58]

Such problems occur with almost all words except perhaps for numbers and especially for words that are universals used to describe resemblances or common attributes shared by particulars. Universals are by necessity vague or indeterminate given that they do not refer to any particular thing by only describe what particular things have in common. The subject of this essay "race" and "class" are universals if they are anything and thus involve such rational problems of vagueness and indeterminancy.

Such word meaning problems however are not limited to universals, but also exist even with the seemingly simple issue of a particular person's self-identity, of individual oneness, and of the Other that is the substance of so much post-modern social justice argument. When they get to words of "self-identity", the post-modern social justice arguments about the meaning of words and language as being social constructs are suddenly forgotten and these words are dogmatically assumed to represent not social constructs but a thing-in-itself that individuals experience privately and then discuss by translation into social construct language. Wittgenstein's Private Language Argument makes clear these arguments are contradictory dogma and perhaps even nonsense because there is no such thing as a private or personal self-identity or oneness in any sense but as a social construct; any talk of a private language known only by an individual speaking is nonsense talk.

Try defining your self-identity in any private language other than by the language you speak. Call yourself "hot", now tell the rest of the word what you mean by this private word "hot" that only you know or speak? Say

---

[58] Wittgenstein, L. *Tractatus Logico-Philosophicus,* 471st edition, translation from the German by C. K. Ogden. Dover Publications: Mineola, NY. (12 January 1998). At §6.342.

"hot" but tell people you mean "cold", does that make any sense? If it is truly a private word of your own creation in no way translated from or translated into a public language, how do you know what you mean by this word?  Or, that what you mean now is the same as what you meant by it yesterday? If there is no social behavior by which to test the word, then either through faulty memory, hallucination, or other error, you may be using your private word differently each time and with different use comes different meaning. As with all words, it is the public or behavior use or usefulness that  defines the meaning of "individual", "self-identity", "oneness", and the "I am" of "I think therefore I am". This is even more conceptually true of the "Other". If we cannot give ourselves a self-identity other than through social identity, we most certainly cannot do it for anything that involves social interaction and of someone that is not us such as the "Other".

The reality about which we use language to communicate may not be a social construct, but the language most certainly is. "I think, therefore I am" is the one undisputable truth in all possible worlds in which we exist, but when it comes to communicating about that "I am", the thinking eventually reaches the point, "whereof one cannot speak, thereof one must be silent"[59].

Regardless of how it may damage our egos, the ego of Toni Morrison and the egos of her feminist readers trying to find their self-identity or oneness, the egos of the gender clueless trying to find their gender, and the egos of pretty much everyone who places too much importance on their self-identity, in language the reality or natural kind of self-identity is that if you want to find or express yourself or give meaning to the words "individual", "oneness", and "self-identity", the only way to do it is by letting others tell you your identity.

Abstractly, the concept that there is no private experience of which we can speak and no private language expressing it that can be translated into any other language is analyzed by Ludwig Wittgenstein's Private Language Argument and is often exemplified by contemplation of the statement "only I know my pain". It is existentially true that only you know the existential nature of your "I am", but unfortunately the unpleasant self-effacing reality is that you only "know" your "pain" through communication and language with

---

[59] Wittgenstein, Ludwig. *Tractatus logico-philosophicus.* translation from the German by C. K. Ogden.  Mineola, NY : Dover Publications. Proposition 7. 471st edition (1998).

others and thus they know your pain as well as you do. 'Pain' as with any word can only be given meaning by observable acts: screaming, clenched muscles or face, blood, ripped muscles, broken bones, taking aspirin, squeezing a ball or biting a bullet, a rising manometer resulting from the squeezing of an air ball; picking a number on a pain chart, and so forth. Though it is existentially true that one can give any or whatever existential meaning one wants to "pain" or any word for that matter, for this same existential reason it is also true that one cannot give any purely private meaning to "pain" or any word because there would be no way to differentiate correct or incorrect meaning — the concept of meaning would become nonsense just as in any wordgame in which contradictions are true everything is true or false however you want it; in a private language the word "meaning" becomes meaningless in anyway but aesthetically. In any imagined private language with private meanings, the concept of meaning would be nonsense because the solitary individual speaker of the private language of private experience would have no way to tell whether or not a word spoken at one time has the same meaning as that same word spoken at any other time. The same would be true of any speakers or observers of any language in which private meanings and a private language are real.

Thus, it is not unfortunate but fortunate there is no such thing as a private language speaking about private sense experience. If there were private languages, there would be no language just gibberish and a cacophony of noise.

**B.**     **<u>The Practical difference Between a Social Construct and an Ontological Fact Is One of Degrees of Pragmatic Value and Not of Substance</u>**

Leaving metaphysics aside and restricting my questions and answers to pragmatic concepts used and useful for social survival, race and class existing in this holistic fabric of language with all other human actions, interactions, and affairs are as much a part of whatever reality exists independent of us as is that independent reality. This may not have been true when humanity was living in caves completely dependent on the universe for survival and may not be true in the future when our descendants become gods as some believe will occur, but for now we are stuck with an intertwined reality of social construction and ontological reality. We have reached the point where the most significant portion of the universe for us consisting of our Earth is as much dependent on our actions, interactions, and affairs to survive as we are on it. Thus, especially for the language of race and class directly involving survival and success for some humans in life at the expense of others in life, social kinds and social construction of concepts dependent on our existence are as real as any natural kind and as any reality independent of our existence. Regardless of what metaphysics might ultimately decide, for purposes of personal survival in society, contemplation of race and class for now and for the foreseeable future involves a holistic ontology in which social constructs are as ontologically real as anything else in reality. This holistic fabric of language, knowledge, and reality was best described by Quine:

> The totality of our so-called knowledge or beliefs, from the most casual matters of geography and history to the profoundest laws of atomic physics or even of pure mathematics and logic, is a man-made fabric which impinges on experience only along the edges. Or, to change the figure, total science is like a field of force whose boundary conditions are experience. A conflict with experience at the periphery occasions readjustments in the interior of the field. Truth values have to be redistributed over some of our statements. Re-evaluation of some statements entails re-evaluation of others, because of their logical interconnections; the logical laws being in turn simply certain further statements of the system, certain further elements of the field. Having re-evaluated one statement we

must re-evaluate some others, whether they be statements logically connected with the first or whether they be the statements of logical connections themselves. But the total field is so undetermined by its boundary conditions, experience, that there is much latitude of choice as to what statements to re-evaluate in the light of any single contrary experience. No particular experiences are linked with any particular statements in the interior of the field, except indirectly through
considerations of equilibrium affecting the field as a whole.

If this view is right, it is misleading to speak of the empirical content of an individual statement, especially if it be a statement at all remote from the experiential periphery of the field. Furthermore it becomes folly to seek a boundary between synthetic statements, which hold contingently on experience, and analytic statements which hold come what may. Any statement can be held true come what may, if we make drastic enough adjustments elsewhere in the system. Even a statement very close to the periphery can be held true in the face of recalcitrant experience by pleading hallucination or by amending certain statements of the kind called logical laws. Conversely, by the same token, no statement is immune to revision. Revision even of the logical law of the excluded middle has been proposed as a means of simplifying quantum mechanics; and what difference is there in principle between such a shift and the shift whereby Kepler superseded Ptolemy, or Einstein Newton, or Darwin Aristotle?

...

As an empiricist I continue to think of the conceptual scheme of science as a tool, ultimately, for predicting future experience in the light of past experience. Physical objects are conceptually imported into the situation as convenient intermediaries -- not by definition in terms of experience, but simply as irreducible posits comparable, epistemologically, to the gods of Homer. Let me interject that for my part I do, *qua* lay physicist, believe in physical objects and not in Homer's gods; and I consider it a scientific error to believe otherwise. But in point of epistemological footing the physical objects and the gods differ only in degree and not in kind. Both sorts of entities enter our conception only as cultural posits. The myth of physical objects is epistemologically superior to most in that it has proved more efficacious than other myths as a device for working a manageable structure into the flux of experience.[60]

The task remaining for this essay is to determine the degrees by which race and class differ but also how they are intertwined in the ontology of human society in which they are both natural and social constructs. From now on, I will dispense with the social construct/ontological reality distinction unless directly at issue because it is distinction that only serves to confuse.

Given this holistic intertwined nature of class and race, to paraphrase Humpty-Dumpty, we get the question: who or what is the master of the weaving of these words race and class into our social fabric?  If we concentrate in the limited area of our social fabric called scientific language, the individual meaning of race and class is a question of their predictive value inferred from the present and thus are ultimately controlled by things as they are: if the use or usefulness of these words cannot give accurate predictions, they eventually will have no scientific meaning and can go the way of words such as phlogiston, ether, and the spinal soul. If we feel along our social fabric away from science onto the humanities especially areas such as politics or even onto the social aspects of science, they become used and useful for  normative language involving questions and answers of what ought to be and thus the words and the speakers of those words start controlling what will be regardless of the present. In this latter normative meaning, often "the label 'social constructionism' is more code than description"[61] for every leftist, Marxist, Freudian, feminist, post-modernist, and social justice questioning of every moral, sex, gender, power, or any other claims with which they disagree. Thus, threading together the predictive and normative meanings for the words "race" and "class" into the holistic fabric of their use and usefulness in human society, their relationship becomes a struggle between the quantitative and material prospering and survival of human society through pragmatic value and its qualitative or normative prospering and survival as a progressive human society. Curing cancer is an obvious example in which pragmatic questions dominate since

---

[60] Quine, W.V.O. (1951). Two dogmas of empiricism. *Philosophical Review, Vol. 60*, Part 1, pp. 35–36. doi: 10.2307/2266637

[61] Hacking, Ian. *The Social Construction of What*, p. 15.

few at the present are normatively against curing cancer. One simple example of the other extreme used by Hacking of this normative aspect is child abuse: is child abuse a real evil or a social construct?[62] At any given time in a culture, no one cares which it is, it is an evil defined morally and ethically regardless of pragmatic value or of degrees of pragmatic value; it is its normative aspects as defined by those who control the words 'child abuse' that control its reality. The problems arise when there is a disputed mixture of pragmatic and normative meanings. The big problems such as socialism or anarchy are obvious, but these disputes occur in the simplest of social problems.

For example, as far as I am concerned, taking a bunch of prepubescent girls away from their parents; sending them to a gymnastics camp; working them 40 hours a week; and then putting them in tights so that they can risk life and limb for the entertainment of adults is child abuse regardless of any benefit to the girls or society. If a bunch of working class parents got together and treated their daughters in such a way, it would be criminal child abuse and illegal child labor and they would lose custody of their kids. Obviously, no one cares what I think nor does anyone do a pragmatic weighting of benefits in order to determine if gymnastics is child abuse or not; it simply is not. Similarly, are race and class used solely as normative code, do they have pragmatic value, or both? Are the masters of the words 'race' and 'class' those who speak them? If so, how far do the speakers control the words and the words control the speakers?

---

[62] Hacking, Ian. *The Social Construction of What*, p. 29.

**IV.     THE PRAGMATIC NECESSITY OF CLASS**

*Throughout recorded time, and probably since the end of the Neolithic Age, there have been three kinds of people in the world, the High, the Middle, and the Low. They have been subdivided in many ways, they have borne countless different names, and their relative numbers, as well as their attitude towards one another, have varied from age to age: but the essential structure of society has never altered. Even after enormous upheavals and seemingly irrevocable changes, the same pattern has always reasserted itself, just as a gyroscope will always return to equilibrium, however far it is pushed one way or the other.*[63]   — George Orwell, *1984.*


I start with a contemplation of class because in the last few decades anyone who has contemplated or studied the existence of social and economic classes agree that "class" in terms of being social construct universal exists and is as real as any universal or particular power that affects humans both individually and socially. In the past history of the United States, there were those who argued the United States is a classless society — more as polemics and politics than as serious scholarly work — but I know of no one at present who has empirically or conceptually studied this question making this argument. In *The Autobiography of An Ex-Colored Man* written in 1912, the author James Johnson described the same class distinctions[64] within black culture that mirrored white culture and thus that existed in all of American society that Thomas Sowell described in *Intellectuals and Race* written in 2013[65]. In *Intellectuals and Race* and other books[66], Sowell goes on to show how the lower class black culture matches

---

[63] Orwell, G. *1984.* p. 201.

[64] Johnson, James W. *The Autobiography of An Ex-Colored Man.* pp. 152-53.

[65] Sowell, Thomas. *Intellectuals and Race.* p. 20.

[66] Sowell, Thomas. *Black Rednecks and White Liberals.* Encouter Books: NY, NY (2005).

not only American lower class white culture — as does other recent books[67]— but also those of other societies such as the British lower working class despite their lack of any recent history of slavery.

The present disagreements on the nature of class are only as to whether there is any meaningful way to define class conceptually for empirical study; as to whether there is class consciousness; as to whether class is earned and fluid across generations or inherited and static; and of course the big disagreement in the United States is the relationship between class and race — are they related and, if so how are they related? I argue that the latter questions are subsidiary or ancillary and do not detract from the reality and power of social class and do not even affect its degree of power in relation to race: class controls race.

Continuing from the beginning quote of this Part IV, Orwell describes the reality of class:

> The aims of these three groups are entirely irreconcilable. The aim of the High is to remain where they are. The aim of the Middle is to change places with the High. The aim of the Low, when they have an aim -- for it is an abiding characteristic of the Low that they are too much crushed by drudgery to be more than intermittently conscious of anything outside their daily lives -- is to abolish all distinctions and create a society in which all men shall be equal. Thus throughout history a struggle which is the same in its main outlines recurs over and over again. For long periods the High seem to be securely in power, but sooner or later there always comes a moment when they lose either their belief in themselves or their capacity to govern efficiently, or both. They are then overthrown by the Middle, who enlist the Low on their side by pretending to them that they are fighting for liberty and justice. As soon as they have reached their objective, the Middle thrust the Low back into their old position of servitude, and themselves become the High. Presently a new Middle group splits off from one of the other groups, or from both of them, and the struggle begins over again. Of the three groups, only the Low are never even temporarily successful in achieving their aims. It would be an exaggeration to say that throughout history there has

---

[67] Isenberg, Nancy. *White Trash: The 400-Year Untold History of Class in America.* Penguin Books: NY, NY. (2016).

been no progress of a material kind. Even today, in a period of decline, the average human being is physically better off than he was a few centuries ago. But no advance in wealth, no softening of manners, no reform or revolution has ever brought human equality a millimeter nearer. From the point of view of the Low, no historic change has ever meant much more than a change in the name of their masters.[68]      — George Orwell, *1984.*

More recently, as a result of a ten-year sociological study with a follow-up study ten years later, the sociologists of *UNEQUAL CHILDHOODS, Class, Race, and Family Life* describe class using the work of the analytic French sociologist Pierre Bourdieu:

> Pierre Bourdieu's work provides a context for examining the impact of social class position. ... Bourdieu argues that individuals of different social locations are socialized differently. This socialization provides children, and later adults, with a sense of what is comfortable or what is natural (he terms this *habitus*). These background experiences also shape the amount and forms of resources *(capital)* individuals inherit and draw upon as they confront various institutional arrangements *(fields)* in the social world.

> ... In any given society, the transmission of privilege is "misrecognized." Individuals tend to see their society's social arrangements as legitimate. Status, privilege, and similar social rewards allegedly are "earned" by individuals; that is, they are perceived as resulting from intelligence, talent, effort, and other strategically displayed skills. Bourdieu, in showing how cultural capital is acquired and used in daily life, makes clear that individuals' social position is not the result of personal attributes such as effort or intelligence. In particular, he argues that individuals in privileged social locations are advantaged in ways that are not a result of the

---

[68] Orwell, G. *1984.* p. 201.

intrinsic merit of their cultural experiences.  Rather, cultural training in the home is awarded unequal value in dominant institutions because of the close compatibility between the standards of child rearing in privileged homes and the (arbitrary) standards proposed by these institutions.

...

Bourdieu also points to nuanced class differences in the interactions between actors and institutions. He notes that people have a wide array of resources, social networks, and cultural training, and that they do not always use all of these resources in all settings. This sensitivity to the complexity and fluidity of social life makes his theory significantly more persuasive than other theories of social inequality, such as a culture of poverty model.

... Bourdieu suggests that differences in habitus give individuals varying cultural skills, social connections, educational practices, and other cultural resources, which then can be translated into different forms of value (i.e., capital) as individuals move out into the world.  It is possible to adopt new habits later in life, but these late-acquired dispositions lack the comfortable (natural) feel associated with those learned in childhood.

The concept of field is crucial.  It encompasses some of the same dynamics captured in terms such as market of social institution. But, as David Swartz points out,  Bourdieu also seeks something broader with the idea of field:  "Bourdieu ...sees the image of 'field' as superior to that of 'institution' for two reasons:  first, he wants to emphasize the conflictual character of social life where the idea of institution suggests consensus; second, he wants a concept that can cover social works where practices are only weakly institutionalized and boundaries are not well established."

Bourdieu argues that in key areas, social space is stratified -- - some groups will be excluded and others included (and some will exclude themselves).  He draws an analogy with a card game:  there are fields that provide both the "rules of the game" and the social space wherein variations in capital exist.  Bourdieu focuses on the intersection of the cards being dealt and the skill with which players play.  He emphasizes that the nature of the game is arbitrary and the slots at the top are limited.  **He would never suggest, for example, that more parents could improve their children's school success by adopting particular practices.  Instead, he would point out that the number of elite slots in society is limited.  Thus, any effort to spread an elite practice to all members of the society would result in the practice being devalued and replaced by a different sorting mechanism.  In this sense, his model suggests that inequality is a perpetual characteristic of social groups.**  In any given interaction, however Bourdieu stresses that the outcome is uncertain.  Strategies may not pay off.  In addition, he notes that individuals with a similar set of resources may differ in the skill with which they use their capital.[69] [emphasis added]

The only challenges to this view of class as a "perpetual characteristic of social groups" is the lack in the modern United States and of most of the modern Western World of explicit class distinctions explicitly enforced by law. From the Roman plebeians, patricians, freemen, and slaves to the pre-French Revolution estates and orders of feudal society and from the lowest tribal distinctions between slaves, warriors, and chiefs to Burmese noblemen, servants, and slaves, class was explicit throughout human history in all human societies in the same way as chattel slavery and was enforced by law in the same way as was chattel slavery. More often than not, such class distinctions were hereditary. Any objection or denial of the existence of modern class social structure based on the lack of its being explicit is a conceptual error. Conceptually, we do not have chattel slavery now because by definition chattel slavery requires explicit treatment of humans as chattel — that is treated as property by law. However, wage slavery can exist without any explicit enforcement or even acknowledgment or recognition of its existence by law or by anyone — simply as a result of economic and

---

[69] Lareau, Annette. *UNEQUAL CHILDHOODS, Class, Race, and Family Life.* University of California Press. 2nd edition. (2011).

social conditions. Similarly, class exists without any explicit enforcement or even acknowledgment or recognition of its existence by law or by anyone — simply as a result of economic and social conditions. George Orwell's storytelling again tracks reality and does a better job of describing it than any social science:

> In principle, membership [in the Party] is not hereditary. The child of Inner Party parents is in theory not born into the Inner Party. ... . Nor is there any racial discrimination, or any marked domination of one province by another. Jews, Negroes, South Americans of pure Indian blood are to be found in the highest ranks of the Party, and the administrators of any area are always drawn from the inhabitants of that area. ... Its rulers are not held together by blood-ties but by adherence to a common doctrine. It is true that our society is stratified, and very rigidly stratified, on what at first sight appear to be hereditary lines. There is far less to-and-fro movement between the different groups than happened under capitalism or even in the pre-industrial age. Between the two branches of the Party there is a certain amount of interchange, but only so much as will ensure that weaklings are excluded from the Inner Party and that ambitious members of the Outer Party are made harmless by allowing them to rise. Proletarians, in practice, are not allowed to graduate into the Party. The most gifted among them, who might possibly become nuclei of discontent, are simply marked down by the Thought Police and eliminated. But this state of affairs is not necessarily permanent, nor is it a matter of principle. The Party is not a class in the old sense of the word. It does not aim at transmitting power to its own children, as such; and if there were no other way of keeping the ablest people at the top, it would be perfectly prepared to recruit an entire new generation from the ranks of the proletariat. In the crucial years, the fact that the Party was not a hereditary body did a great deal to neutralize opposition. The older kind of Socialist, who had been trained to fight against something called 'class privilege' assumed that what is not hereditary cannot be permanent. He did not see that the continuity of an oligarchy need not be physical, nor did he pause to reflect that hereditary aristocracies have always been

shortlived, whereas adoptive organizations such as the Catholic Church have sometimes lasted for hundreds or thousands of years. The essence of oligarchical rule is not father-to-son inheritance, but the persistence of a certain world-view and a certain way of life, imposed by the dead upon the living. A ruling group is a ruling group so long as it can nominate its successors. The Party is not concerned with perpetuating its blood but with perpetuating itself. Who wields power is not important, provided that the hierarchical structure remains the same.[70]

The real dispute is not whether class exists but whether class unlike chattel slavery (but perhaps like wage slavery?) is a necessary result and attribute of any human society?

The only serious objection to the existence of social classes is the lack or agreement of any explicit or even implicit definition of class that has pragmatic or predictive meaning — many argue the concept is so vague that it can be used to apply to any social inequality.

First, being vague is not a sound or valid objection in the modern world to the pragmatic or predictive value of a word. Science is dependent on vague words for its explanatory powers especially for its mathematical concepts because very few can do the math. An example is the 'c' of $E = mc^2$ contemplated previously but there are many others. "'It is important to realize that in physics today we have no knowledge of what energy is', said Richard Feynman in his *Lectures* in the Sixties. 'Nobody knows what energy really is' can be read in Bergmann and Schaefer's Experimental Physics, 1998"[71]. Entropy has an even more humble or infamous beginning; it is essentially a name given to the unexplainable remainder occurring in thermodynamics equations. No one knows what entropy is, yet it is in anything that wants to call itself a science. Information science is illustrative:

---

[70] Orwell, G. *1984*. p. 208-09.

[71] Coelho, Ricardo L. "On the concept of energy: History and philosophy for science teaching". *Procedia Social and Behavioral Sciences* 1 (2009) p. 2648.

I thought of calling it "information", but the word was overly used, so I decided to call it "uncertainty". [...] Von Neumann told me, "You should call it entropy, for two reasons. In the first place your uncertainty function has been used in statistical mechanics under that name, so it already has a name. In the second place, and more important, nobody knows what entropy really is, so in a debate you will always have the advantage.
— Conversation between Claude Shannon and John von Neumann regarding what name to give to the attenuation in phone-line signals.[72]

No scientist has ever seen nor will they see a "photon", but they have seen what experiments are conducted and what data appears on experimental equipment for which that word is used:

Although I'm often guilty of it myself, I think it's a little misleading for physicists to keep harping on about 'wave-like' and 'particle-like' behavior," he wrote. "We have a great mathematical theory which tells us what photons ... actually do. And then we have the human tendency to draw analogies and say 'hmm, in this case that looks like what I expect from a water wave' and 'but in this case that looks like what I expect from a billiard ball.' But photons are neither water waves nor billiard balls. ...

... If two ripples cross in a pool, and I reach a cupped hand in and pull out a handful of water to ask you 'which ripple are these water molecules from?' there is no answer.

There is no answer because it's not a well-posed question, not because there is any deep mystery to the physics of water waves. ...

---

[72] Tribus, M.; McIrvine, E.C. "Energy and information". *Scientific American*, 224 (September 1971), pp. 178–184.

In the end, quantum mechanics is the same. When you ask careful, experimentally testable questions, there is no paradox. ...

What it teaches us is that we haven't yet figured out how to think about quantum mechanics right – not that there is any problem with the theory itself or how we use it to make predictions.[73]

If science can use vague words for an understanding of reality as long as they give  pragmatic or predictive meaning, there is no reason why vague words cannot be used for an understanding of the pragmatic and normative reality of class.

Second, there is no need to be so vague as to make the word 'class' apply to any inequality because there is an implicit definition in all language and empirical study of class that is not made explicit because all such study and language is created by the upper classes or their intelligentsia. Only they have the power to study it and to create its language. They do not see the definition because they are it or a part of it in the same way none of us see infrared and other so-called invisible light despite some animals being able to see it and despite being surrounded by it: it is not visible to us until we have the instrumental need to create an ability to see it. I will argue later that the only reason academia and its intelligentsia are now starting to be aware of and to study class is because in modern Technological Society they — as with most of the middle class — are starting to join the working class instead of being above it.

Based on my life experience varying from the drudgery of illiterate working class life to the intellectual heights of Harvard and NYU, I propose to make it explicit: class is the degree by which any individual in a social group or by which subgroups of individuals in a social group have the power

---

[73] Ben P. Stein, Aephraim Steinberg. *No, You Cannot Catch An Individual Photon Acting Simultaneously As A Pure Particle And Wave.* Inside Science (2015); https://www.insidescience.org/news/no-you-cannot-catch-individual-photon-acting-simultaneously-pure -particle-and-wave

to control the normative language of the entire group — it is the power to decide what the entire group normatively ought to be or do. Class is the power to decide ethics. Degrees of this power decide one's class. As much as I disagree with Marxism, Marx's critique that ethics is ruling class ideology was directly on-point. This definition has pragmatic and predictive meaning for all and across all social groups, from the smallest street gang to the most complex.

The question of whether the power that defines class is based on the means of production or upon the dialectical logic of a Word Spirit is beyond the scope of this essay as I have left metaphysics behind for this essay. I am seeking practical answers to a practical question of survival. This essay and definition result from my >50 years of life experience contemplating race and class. I have as much right to define class as a sociologist studying it for ten years and, furthermore, to ask whether class as defined is a necessary attribute of human society.

Based on everything I have read and experienced, class is a necessary attribute of any large social group. The delineation of how large must await another day, but it does not take too many. Even in a group of three, class might exist if the struggle for power is too one-sided and held by one individual. The presence of class is unavoidable in order to fight against any group's and humanity's ultimate and universal enemy: nature and its indifference at best but usually antagonism to our existence. One of the side effects or outright delusions that the power of Technological Society has given humanity is losing sight of this battle. A tsunami drowns 15,000 people and causes a nuclear reactor meltdown, yet the social justice humanities only complain about the meltdown that killed no one and injured three but somehow these supposed humanitarians are still in love with the beauty of nature that killed 15,000. As in any battle, victory requires organization, discipline, the will to fight, and luck. Nothing we can do about luck, except as the Romans used to say "*audentes fortuna juvat*" (Fortune favors the brave). Class serves to give us the organization and discipline needed for this battle.

Our will to fight those who have power over us or who want power over us, regardless of whether it is internal to our social group or an attack from the outside, is supposed to assure our ruling class gives us the necessary organization and discipline needed to win our battles with the universe. The

Powers are not supposed just to seek or to be power as an end in itself and thus become a traitor to the power of our opponent consisting of the power of nature. I have written more extensively about this in my essay contemplating an *Existential Philosophy of Law*[74] and will return to contemplation of this conclusion in my final analysis and conclusion here.

---

[74]

https://papers.ssrn.com/sol3/papers.cfm?abstract_id =3008894

## V.        WHAT IS RACE?


*The gods mercifully gave mankind this little moment of peace between the religious fanaticisms of the past and the fanaticisms of class and race that were speedily to arise and dominate time to come.*[75]

— G.M. Trevelyan


The above quote is used by Thomas Sowell as an epigram to begin his book *Intellectuals and Race* and refers to the historical period known as The Enlightenment running roughly between the year 1700 and the French Revolution. This quote exhibits an overly optimistic view of The Enlightenment and an overly pessimistic view of the prior period of supposed "fanaticism". It is the struggle between Christianity and the secular state for power and the resulting power balance it created that gave us Western Civilization; without it we would be no better than the history of state worship that is Eastern Civilization. Now that Christianity has surrendered to the state and the state has subsumed Christian values but without the Christianity to get it an empathic soul at least, state worship is returning through post modern social justice promises of a Hegelian utopia but I do not see it giving us an Enlightenment; by effects such as the killing of history, a disenlightenment is the more likely result.[76] Furthermore, the Enlightenment saw its fair share of wars raging from the Lithuanian Civil War to our own Revolutionary War. Without the historical effects of the

---

[75] Trevelyan, G.M. *English Social History: A Survey of Six Centuries, Chaucer to Queen Victoria*. Longmans, Green and Co.: London (1942) p. 339.

[76] I wrote a separate essay on this problem, *Why Tolerate Law*. https://papers.ssrn.com/sol3/papers.cfm?abstract_id =2948585

latter and those of the French Revolution, much of the ideas of the Enlightenment would never have passed into practice.

However, the quote does serve to highlight the reversion of historical struggle in Western Civilization from religious struggle that subsumed within it race and class struggle to a return of the ancient struggle between race and class of which the Ancients were honest about and acknowledged by their laws and traditions explicitly recognizing both class and race. For the Ancients however, "race" was synonymous to our words for ethnicity, nation, or tribe and not limited solely to the present dispute of race defined by blackness and whiteness. Ethnicity in pre-modern times was the same as "race". All modern ethnicities from Albanian to Zulu are the creations of struggles usually in the form of war. If struggle created race, it did so in the same way it created all ancestral, tribal, national, ethnic, some religious identities such as the Jewish Nation, language differences, and similar cultural and social distinctions among humans in life. We would not have Italian, German, Serbian, Jewish, or any ethnicities and nations, tribes, people, or whatever without the conflicts that either united or separated them into their respective differences. The whole racist argument for the existence of a superior German or Aryan nation was based on their millennia existence as the first line of defense for Europe against attacking Asian "hordes". Just as "struggle" has supposedly created Coates' "black bodies" and black "race" and the reality, unity, and language of his black "people" and "tribe", it has created all bodies, peoples, and tribes regardless of whether we call the differences cultural, social, ancestry, population, or any acceptable version of 'race'.

What is race in our Technological Society? Is it or will it be subsumed into class struggle in the same way class struggle was subsumed into the religious struggle of our past or is it a separate struggle?

Unfortunately, because history is dead, it cannot help us with these questions except as I stated earlier to counteract the citation to history by post-modernism and social justice warriors. Unlike class, even now the meaning of race is relatively simple: "a set of people genetically and indelibly different from others in physical characteristics of one sort or another".[77] However, once our fingers pass this defining tread and feel onto the remainder of our social fabric, the threads get hopelessly muddled, coarse, lost, and outright broken, loose, and tangled at best, at worse they get retreaded with no definitions. This is not only true among popular and political disputes on the topic of race but even among the supposedly most educated and supposedly the most intelligent. At present and for the foreseeable future, it is impossible to talk about race in this country. One of the reasons for it being so is the many books written by academics on race that start out with the social justice premise that all history is fiction then proceed to prove their premise through fiction seeking to reach a predetermined conclusion about race usually without even bothering to define race — or class. It is simply not worthwhile to read anything called "empirical" on race written by academics anymore.

It is worse when they use statistical correlations in their books. One can find a statistical correlation for anything if one looks hard enough[78]. The key to interpreting statistical correlations and distinguishing spurious from material is life experience and pragmatism not a normative theory of ethics and morality that will always seek to confirm itself. Since most humanities and so-called social science academics come from class backgrounds that gave them the time and money to spend years in academia gaining acceptance by their academic peers, lacking life experience seems to be one of the required prerequisites for being an esteemed humanities academic, thus interpretation of mathematics and statistics is not going to be one of their abilities. This gets worse as their careers proceed, "[a] crucial fact about the theories and social visions of intellectuals is that the intelligentsia pay no

---

[77] Sowell, Thomas. *Intellectuals and Race.* p. 1.

[78] *See* http://www.tylervigen.com/spurious-correlations for such great correlations as "The number of people who drowned by falling into a pool correlates with films Nicholas Cage appeared in".

price for being wrong"[79]. *"Don't ape the natural sciences"*[80] is the physicists' Alan Sokal and Jean Bricmont's admonition in their book <u>Fashionable Nonsense</u> to the humanities and so-called social sciences but it has fallen on death ears. (Doubt most academic writers on race and class can do the math. They seem to have others create the correlations they need and then incorporate them into their polemics.) Following are some examples.

In the book *Toxic Inequality* written by a highly esteemed supposed expert on race relations Thomas M. Shapiro, I did not make it past the introduction without finding a material misrepresentation of fact[81]. In it he writes that banks such as Countrywide and others "stipulated" to race discrimination in lending as part of their settlement agreements with the Department of Justice and actually cited to the government webpages with the settlement agreements. I actually looked up the agreements because based on prior experience with such settlements I knew they always stipulate to the opposite: the settlement is not an admission of liability. As always, the cited agreements after repeating the governments' allegations stipulated the settlement was not an admission of liability. As always, to save litigation expenses, the banks settle for pennies on the dollar and the AG gets political brownie points without anything ever being proved or admitted. The writers did not bother to look up the cited agreements and they probably knew the readers never would. The book is full of such gamesmanship. Shapiro is a fiction writer in the post-modern and social justice sense of history as fiction.

In *The Wages of Whiteness: Race and the Making of the American Working Class* written by another supposed expert David R. Roediger, history as fiction reaches a point of being bad fiction yet still sells. Even fiction is at least supposed to have characters that make sense even if the facts do not; the characters are supposed to be real human beings or at least reveal the complex soul of humanity not just be cartoons — in this book, they are not even colorful cartoons just black and white cartoons. This book

---

[79] Sowell, Thomas. *Intellectuals and Race.* p. 136.

[80] Sokal, Alan; Bricmont, Jean. *Fashionable Nonsense.* N.Y., N.Y.: Picador (1999) p. 187.

[81] Shapiro, Thomas M. *Toxic Inequality.* Basic Books: N.Y. (2017). p. 9.

seems to have made the cartoon concept of "Whiteness" enter mainstream —
probably in the same way the television show *Vampire Diaries* made
vampires mainstream instead of the high art of political and social
commentary that is Bram Stoker's *Dracula*. According to Roediger, all
discrimination or struggle suffered by any minority in the United States and
seemingly the world during the last two hundred years was caused by
Whiteness and was resolved only when the minority became or embraced
Whiteness. "Whiteness" for the humanities has become an empirical
universal as real as universals such as energy, torque, matter, and light;
supposedly, Whiteness is responsible for all modern misery but that
somehow despite being so powerful and omnipresent is not responsible for
any of the benefits of modern living that came into existence during those
same two hundred years such as the elimination of chattel slavery for the first
time in human history. Of course, he never bothers to contemplate the
metaphysical nature of universals and uses various definitions of race and
class as needed to create Whiteness. It is not possible to argue with such
fanaticism.

An epitome of the writing regularly published by academics that
makes rational discourse on race impossible is the book *Color Conscious*. It
is sad that a book such as this is written by K. Anthony Appiah, the head of a
philosophy department at a world university such as NYU, and by Amy
Gutmann, the President of the University of Pennsylvania.

The first half of this book is written by Appiah in which he argues
not that "race" ought not as a matter of normative belief be used by science
regardless of any scientific meaning it may have as any educated individual
may be allowed to argue but argues instead that it has no scientific meaning;
thus he indirectly disproves my point that history does not repeat itself — in
rare circumstances it does. The non-scientist intellectuals and
pseudointellectuals in the early 20th Century varying from Adolf Hitler to
Woodrow Wilson, though unable to do the science themselves and lacking
any understanding of the limitations of the scientific wordgame, grabbed
onto the fledgling science of genetics to create the now ridiculed cult of
eugenics to satisfy the prevailing overarching vision among intellectuals: a
preference for a society guided from the top down by ideas inspired by
intellectual elites. Now their descendants in early 21st Century intelligentsia,
while still unable to do the science themselves and while not understanding

the potential of the scientific wordgame, ridicule genetic scientists for using statistical mathematics involving the word "race". Why is a philosopher who is not even a philosopher of science lecturing to science, to scientists, to the public, and to politicians on what are or should be practical scientific terms? Even if Appiah was a philosopher of science, this at best would allow him to critique science as a part of ontology and epistemology but still not lecture on how to do science. As the physicist Richard Feynman supposedly said, "the philosophy of science is as useful to scientists as ornithology is to birds." At least Kate Clancy was honest enough to admit she was stifling fellow scientist Watson's scientific language on ethical and moral grounds she considered more important than science. As he claims to be an expert on ethics and moral philosophy, Appiah should have the decency to admit the same. In fact, he seems to have given up entirely on writing serious philosophical work instead to write a Dear Abby type column for rich people in the New York Times called "The Ethicist" answering their trendy and usually outright silly questions pretending to care about ethics — once again proving the historical lesson that ethics is no more than ruling class ideology. Religion may be the opiate of the masses but thanks to intelligentsia such as Appiah, ethics is the opiate or aspirin of the rich and powerful that eliminates any headaches caused by their will for power — other than the pill of satisfaction.

In the present holistic fabric of scientific knowledge in which epigenetics has challenged the "Central Dogma of Molecular Biology" that DNA makes RNA makes protein by discovering evidence that environment can violate the irreversible attribute of the Dogma and even change inheritable traits directly, something that is supposed to be a genetic impossibility[82], it is as ludicrous to say any universal word with such a long

---

[82] Buchanan, Anne V.; Sholtis, Samuel; *et al.* "What are genes "for" or where are traits "from"? What is the question?" *Bioessays* (February 2009), p. 3-4, 10-12. doi: 10.1002/bies.200800133. Gerstein, Mark B.; Bruce, Can; Rozowsky, Joel S.; *et al.* "What is a gene, post-ENCODE? History and updated definition". *Genome Res.* (2007) Vol. 17, p. 670. doi:

history of use as "race" can have no meaning in science as it would be to say "population", "ancestry", "heritage", or even Coates' favorite words to define his "people" such as "tribe", "black bodies", or "Blackness" have no meaning nor useful meaning. If "Whiteness" is a meaningful word to describe an aspect of reality, "race" most certainly is. Appiah seems to have no understanding of the nature of the scientific wordgame and seems to truly believe there is a substantive difference --- not just an aesthetic difference --- between saying statistical "population" and statistical "race". Or, is he simply pretending to do so as a political image to satisfy ambitions for further academic advancement? Like Clancy, what Appiah is really doing is making a normative argument against the use of the word "race" that converts a concept of acceptable etiquette into one of ontology. The word 'race' has connotations of slavery. So, instead of saying the "race" of Ashkenazi Jews has a high frequency of certain genetic diseases or the Black "race" in the United States has a high frequency of asthma, a scientist ought to say the "population" or "ancestry" of Ashkenazi Jews has a high frequency of certain genetic diseases and that the population of Black Americans in the United States have a high frequency of asthma. Would it not be racist and evidence of "Whiteness" for scientists to ignore a genetic trait for asthma in the population of Black Americans that may result from the epigenetics of environment? Thus, the brilliant minds of Clancy and Appiah as masters of the words have changed what should be a rational scientific dispute on the predictive meaning of universals into an argument over proper table etiquette.

President Gutman in the second half of her book with Appiah proposes to replace "race" with "color conscious". I can just imagine her and other academics in a conference room with some skin color charts deciding whose skin color will justify their academic *noblesse oblige* and whose will

---

10.1101/gr.6339607. Strohman, Richard C. "Epigenesis and Complexity, The Coming Kuhian revolution in biology". *Nature Biotechnology*. Vol. 15 (March 1997) p. 195. Woese, Carl R. "A New Biology for a New Century". *Microbiology and Molecular Biology Reviews*. June, 2004, p. 175. DOI: 10.1128/MMBR.68.2.173-186.2004.

not warrant it. This is their solution for racism? So, my daughter is half Black and half White; is she worthy of their color consciousness? How about if she were 1/8 Black, 1/16? How will they decide? It cannot be according to class because according to them race trumps class as the greater evil. Also, they cannot use genetics because genetically there is no race. Could one use self-reporting such as Elizabeth Warren reporting she is 1/32 Cherokee or whatever she said? This has obvious problems if you are going to be handing out scholarships, jobs, money, and other preferences based on color consciousness. It seems the success of her solution for racism will be to become obsessed with ancestry records as was Nazi jurisprudence and legal culture when trying to differentiate their Aryan *Herrenvolk* or master race of the *Volksgemeinschaft* or "people's community" from their slave Non-Aryan races such as Jews, Romani, Slavs, Poles, Serbs, Blacks, and so forth. So, for example, some in the Nazi legal culture argued one was Jewish if one was only 1/16 Jewish blood. Eventually, the criterion for being Jewish was set at having at least three Jewish grandparents; two or one rendered a person a *Mischling* leaving open the possibility of your extermination to the discretion, mercy, and wisdom of the judiciary. These standards became law in the same way anything becomes law: through the arbitrary and random ethics or will for power decisions of a bunch of bureaucrats. So, Gutman, whose parents came to this country to avoid Nazi jurisprudence and Nazi race consciousness will have to use it to establish and enforce "color conscious"? As the master of the words, she changes them but keeps the meaning the same; she replaces substance by etiquette.

Thomas Sowell has done an excellent analysis of the absurdity of the present absence of any shared language to discuss race in his book *Intellectuals and Race*. There is no need for me to go further into this conceptual problem in order to get some answers to my present contemplation. Rather, it is time again to seek answers not in abstraction but in particulars including the particulars of my life experience varying from lower working class to the Olympus of Harvard Law and from the inspiration of the previously mentioned, almost forgotten great book: *Black No More* by the Black-American writer George S. Schulyer.

       **The Problem of Rachel Dolezale and the Answer It Gives to My Questions**

Mr. Schuyler's novel *Black No More* was partially science fiction but mainly and substantively a study of human nature. His premise was that medical technology had developed the ability to make black skin white so black people could become white people. I will not give away the events nor end of the story, but the science fiction portion of the story should no longer be considered fiction. Just as science can change the physical attributes of gender, generate clones, grow biological organs, and much more, science through techniques such as cosmetic surgery and genetic engineering will soon be able to make 'people of color' of whatever color they want: white, black, or anything in between so that a white person need be 'white no more' and a black person need be 'black no more'. Then what? Will technology finally end racism? Or, will this technology only make it worse by allowing Whiteness to further oppress Blackness and to oppress natural 'black' bodies from 'white' society?

The certainty of this technology helps create the language that is missing for resolving the conceptual questions about our society's use and the usefulness of the words 'racism', 'race', 'whiteness', and 'black'. In using my hypothetical technological scenario to get a better understanding of human nature in general and in particular race and racism, in order for this to be honest contemplation, one must be clear and honest as to the pragmatic nature of technology: it does not care about our ethics or morality, it simply wants to work efficiently.

This contemplation partially came up and its issues became real a few years ago with the events of Rachel Dolezal, the former leader of the Spokane, Washington, NAACP chapter. She is the former head because the NAACP discovered she was white: both parents were listed as Caucasian on her Montana birth certificate and all her known ancestors had a complete Caucasian descent of mixed Czech, German, and Swedish origin. She did attend and graduate in four years from Howard University, described by the writer Ta-Nehisi Coates in his book *Between the World and Me* as the "black Mecca" though he was not able to graduate from there despite five years of trying. She eventually admitted she was born "white" but considered herself "black"; she "identified as black" and felt constrained by the "biological identity thrust upon her"[83]. Clearly, she did not consider being 'black' to be solely a sense experience issue of skin color but a social construct, and she wanted in on it. As easily could have been predicted, she was universally condemned by academia and postmodern social justice warriors as a poser and wigger and forced to resign. The liberal and feminist philosophers who provide the philosophical intellectual foundation for female individual identity gender orientation constructs such as transgender, third gender, genderqueer, and other terms they create were unwilling to honestly take their logic to its necessary conclusion in Dolezal's case.

Why were they unwilling to do so? Unlike sexual identity, ethnicity and race, social justice theory and its worshipers do not care about what Dolezal may or may not "think" about her identity. To what extent if at all does being "black" define more than just genetic skin color but also a social and cultural group of exclusive membership to those born with black skin or is it exclusive membership into what? Why is 'wigger' considered to be a derogatory term while words such as 'Italian-American' or 'Irish American' are not? A wigger is a white person who tries to emulate or acquire cultural behavior and tastes attributed to black people. Seems fairly harmless, yet it is not. Why Not? This problem gets exponentially worse when we throw in persons of mixed heritage. If one out of two parents is black, is the child black? One out of four grandparents? One out of eight great grandparents? So forth? Only if the child looks black? Why do we have such a word as 'Italian-American' that has usually good but some bad connotations yet no word for mixed white-black Americans other than mixed or people of color? How much color is necessary to make a person a 'person of color'? Being a black person is a basis for claiming illegal discrimination and oppression by white persons in the United States. Why was Dolezal not commended for her attempts to join an oppressed group? If she called herself Tibetan and joined a bunch of Buddhist monks in a hunger strike against China, she would be commended; how is calling herself black and joining them in their battle

---

[83]

http://www.mirror.co.uk/news/world-news/rachel-d olezal-disgraced-race-activist-5894315 against oppression any different? If she moved to Italy, learned Italian, and lived Italian culture, she could honestly call herself Italian without the Italians complaining; in fact it would be a compliment for Italy for an American to want to be Italian just as it is the United States when immigrants such as me call ourselves American even though we were not born in or into the United States.

If Dolezale were born in Italy of Italian parents, spoke Italian, and lived as an Italian most of her childhood and adult life, could she call herself an Italian-American and even an American (especially once she gets her formal citizenship) by simply moving to Brooklyn, learning to speak American, and accepting and living American culture, ideology, and values? Sure, this is what many immigrants have done and are doing. If an Italian lives in Brooklyn, engages in only American cultural activity, believes in the sovereignty of the United States, is a patriot of the United States, becomes an American citizen, acts American, speaks American, and believes in American values, should they be terminated from employment for calling themselves Italian-American instead of Italian or even for calling themselves American? No. In fact, terminating them for such a reason would be a violation of state and federal anti-discrimination law forced upon society by the Powers. This ability to convert ethnic identity is true of all modern Western ethnic, tribal, national, religious, and ethnicities (the old school Ancient "races" created by different forms of old school racist struggle) unless you are a racist or right-wing fanatic who believes in the purity of ethnicities. In which case, the differences are permanent because racists want such truth in the same way all racists want their arbitrary, invalid, unsound generalizations to be true.

Dolezal never claimed she had black skin, she was claiming to be "black". Other people than assumed she had some shade of black skin or had black ancestors — why did they make that assumption? What if she claimed to be African-American? There are plenty of white African-Americans — whites born or descended from whites born in Africa. For her, such a claim would most definitely have been fraud and not the same as "black" because she was not born nor had any known relatives born in Africa, yet the same would be true of many black Americans that prefer to be called 'African-American' and are so-called. How is the meaning of the word 'black' in 'black person' distinct from the word 'black' in the words 'black skin'?

At present and in the foreseeable future, no matter how Dolezale changes our "color conscious" sense experience of her and regardless of the existential purgatory in which she may in fact reside because of Despair and lack of Authenticity, she will never be perceived as black. If she undergoes successful DNA engineering to actually make her skin the blackest of black (a technique that will no doubt be available in the near future), this will only turn any perception of her as a harmless eccentric to a racist putting on black face. She could trace her ancestry far enough back so as to find multiple slave ancestors of different race and ethnic backgrounds because we would all be able to find them in our ancestry if we wanted given the omnipresence of slavery in all history. However, such a tracing would make matters worse for her; she would then be perceived as a racist guilty of cultural misappropriation. Regardless of her individuality, her self-identity, or her life experience, she will always be perceived as white; she was born white and will die white — unless post-modernist social justice allows her to be black.

Even through just a casual inspection of the language involved with Dolezale, we can see the intertwined holistic fabric of language at work. Somewhere in human history, there may be a thread of the fabric of racist language in which white skinned people for the first time physically met black skinned people and for the first time used the word 'race' as a differentiation between white-skinned and black-skinned bodies. Whenever that first thread stitching occurred, it is now lost among millions of other threads in language and perhaps was removed and retreaded and is gone. This is evident even in the simplest uses of the words 'race' and 'racism'.

For example, the Plaintiff Plessy in the post Civil War 19th Century Supreme Court case of *Plessy v. Ferguson* that established the separate but equal doctrine of Jim Crow laws was an octoroon, he was only 1/8 black by birth and could have easily passed and did pass as white — he could have and did ride in the front of the train in the segregated Old South any time he wanted. That is why he was chosen as the Plaintiff for that case. The Plaintiff Counsel were trying to show how irrational the concept of race was and that therefore how irrational and thus unconstitutional legally enforced segregation must be. The Supremes disagreed. Even before the 19th Century, the word 'race' for racists had uses way beyond just for reference to someone having 'black' skin. If Plessy was 'black' because one of his eight parents/grandparents was black, what about if he was 1/16 black? How far back does or should a racist go to define race? It is evident that for racists, words such as 'race', 'racist', and 'black' mean much more than skin color. The masters of these words use them to create a word reality of social and cultural relations much of which has little if any relation to empirical reality but is just as real.

How this word reality becomes more powerful than reality and in fact contorts reality to fit the words is evident in the previously discussed obsession by Nazi jurisprudence and legal culture to differentiate their Aryan *Herrenvolk* or master race of the *Volksgemeinschaft* or "people's community" from their slave Non-Aryan races such as Jews, Romani, Slavs, Poles, Serbs, Blacks, and so forth.

I am using a hypothetical scenario on whether technology will provide the solution to racism, either real or imagined, to get a better understanding of human nature and the present nature of racism, both old school and new school racism. Once the cosmetic surgery or genetic engineering of a "White No More" or "Black No More" becomes widespread allowing skin color to be just another fashion decision for adults and a parental choice of attributes for babies, people will be whatever skin color they want and therefore racism should disappear. After all, once there is no such thing as genetically decided permanent skin color anymore, people will no longer be able to place anyone in any white or black race category based on sense experience skin color. Or will they? The logic seems simple enough but the events of Rachel Dolezal show it may not be that easy. It is easy enough to determine why racists would want her to lose her job, but why supposed non-racists wanted her — a single mother with two kids to support with one of those kids the son of a black ex-husband and thus definitely black by social justice standards — to be unemployed is confusing and difficult to grasp.

To a racist living the delusion of a genetically socially and culturally superior white race and an inferior black race, Dolezal was a fraud and a traitor to her true superior white color by pretending to be an inferior black; thus, she should be punished by the loss of her job. A racist might also argue that as a fraud and traitor, she deserves to live and work with the inferior black race and thus let this loser keep her job; essentially expel her from the 'white' race. Either way, the reasoning is based on their delusion of white supremacy and black inferiority. To a racist, Dolezal's qualifications, competency, education, and job performance are irrelevant to deciding her fate, the only material issues are skin color and the appropriate punishment for her denial of her "true" skin color that is physically associated with the superior attributes of whiteness.

Our predicted technology would be able to eliminate this old school racism because there will be no "true" skin color to betray nor to misrepresent and thus no superior or inferior attributes to be associated with any particular skin color. Once being white or black is not a genetic attribute firmly established at conception, a racist will eventually lose the ability to make racist associations and until then will lose the ability to do anything about any racist associations they do make because they will not know who is truly white or black by their or their relatives' physical appearance. Saying a person is black and therefore inferior so that one can discriminate against or oppress that person because the person is full, ½, 1/4, 1/8, or whatever 'black' is useless if the full, ½, 1/4, 1/8, or whatever 'black' may in fact be all white and the same is true of the converse. The best they would be able to do would be to discriminate against and oppress people who choose to have black skin and thus the issue of whether they are full, ½, 1/4, 1/8, or whatever black is irrelevant, the only relevant fact would be their fashion choice of skin color. There would be no white or black 'race' but only sense experience of white or back skin — which is the situation we want or should want, supposedly.

This latter situation is substantively not racism but a new type of -ism. It is not discrimination and oppression of persons who are of a 'black' race but of persons who choose to wear a certain fashion or cosmetic trend. It would be the same as discriminating against persons who have breast enhancement, nose jobs, wear bow ties, wear white after Labor Day, or any of the infinite number of ways people discriminate against each other because they do not like each other or view each other as inferior to them. It would not be an issue of a superior 'white' race and an inferior 'black' race, but simply of a superior or inferior fashion style.

It may be understandable why a non-racist may consider Dolezal a fraud but not a traitor since supposedly to them there really is no 'race' to betray. As far as they are concerned, she is a physically white person pretending to be a physically black person in the same way that a sighted person would be a fraud pretending to be blind or a physically healthy person pretending to be disabled in order to get handicap parking stickers would be a fraud — or the other way around. To a supposed non-racist, the supposed important fact is that she lied about her skin color or pretended to be black when she is not; she was a wigger, which is a bad thing. Thus a non-racist would conclude Dolezal deserves to lose her job for being a fraud regardless of her qualifications, competency, education, and job performance in the same way that any employee lying to their employer should lose their job based on fraud — regardless of whether or not she really believes or identifies with being black. To a supposed non-racist, her identification as black is simply a sign of mental illness, such as a hypochondriac who is not ill always believing she is ill only in her case she did not believe in an illness but in being a skin color she was not.

In the latter case of supposed non-racist reasoning, where supposedly there is no racism, our technology should at least be able to keep Dolezal employed at the NAACP, right? Assume she goes to "White No More", views their choice of skin colors from Plessy Black (in honor of the octoroon from <u>Plessy v. Ferguson</u> who could pass as white) to Zulu Black (their darkest available color), and she chooses Zulu Black. She then does the surgery/genetic engineering at her own expense and is now of Zulu Black skin color. She can now honestly apply for employment at the NAACP, tell them she is black since they seem to care, and honestly get employment as a black person, right?

That should be the case based on the supposed non-racist logic for throwing her out into the street, but it does not seem to be the case. Such a color change would be called "putting on black face" and is considered more racist that being a wigger. This is where I lose the logic of the fraud basis for making her lose her employment. If someone was only pretending to be blind but is then blinded, they are no longer pretending, they are blind. What is different about the supposed non-racist definition for supposedly nonexistent 'race' and its relation to the sense experience of skin color that does not allow for a person of physical white skin to become a person of physically black skin — or the other way — without being called racist?

The answer as to why the single mother Dolezale should be thrown into the street is found in the self-serving logic of the supposed non-racist

Ta-Nehisi Coates and his many worshipers who wanted Dolezal unemployed. According to them, racism and whatever language it creates are creations by racist 'white' people or through their white supremacy 'Whiteness' view of the world. The two-way street of racist language is not true of their supposedly non-racist language; they claim to see reality as it really is, not as their words make it out to be as they state racists do. Coates is considered a genius by describing the situation as follows: "race is the child of racism, not the father." By "race" and "racism", he is not referring to the use of those words in several millennia of different applications that include tribal, religious, ethnic, national, and many other differences but only as used in his self-centered narrow view of the world consisting of "race" and "racism" based on skin color. According to this line of thought, we will never be able to eliminate the discrimination and oppression of physically perceived black bodies by physically perceived white bodies because of the ongoing legacy of slavery and of a white supremacy view of history, the present and the future that are Whiteness. Thus, their argument is that being 'black' is by definition a skin color but also an oppressed 'race' forced to accept racism and race as a fact of life.

If "race" truly "is the child of racism, not the father", cannot the father die and we would still have the son that is "race"? This seems to be the implication and is how this thought plays out in practice to create what I will call new school racism.

So, for supposed non-racists such as Coates just as for old school racists, being black connotes both a sense experience skin color and also a cultural and inherited social identity that is called being 'black'. Coates further complains that the "black bodies" created by racism are in need of protection from those who call themselves "white"; of whites casting of him and his "people" into a black "race" that knowingly glance at each other at airports and know they share a special bond; and of the reality, unity, and language of his black "people" and "tribe". Unlike racists though, for supposed non-racist Coates and his worshipers this 'race' identity is defined not solely by skin color but by skin color combined with oppression, slavery, and discrimination by whites based on black skin color. He need not get into issues of mixed heritage; his focus is completely self-centered into a simple white and black distinction: white is bad; black is good. This is why they avoid asking the question of how many black ancestors are required for a person to call themselves a 'black' body because such question will obviously and clearly put them into the position of the racist trying to decide whether 1/32, 1/16 or 1/8 Jewish blood is enough to make one Jewish. They try to ignore their use of the word 'race' and thus its meaning because they want to pretend they are not racists. Like Roediger, Coates and social justice theory need not treat persons as colorful cartoons, just black and white ones.

The logic is as follows: white people by their white supremacy oppression and discrimination of black bodies, especially through slavery, created and create anew every day "black bodies", and a black "people", "tribe", or "race" that are now in need of protection from this oppression and discrimination by the power of Whiteness, therefore white people such as Dolezal should not be allowed to pretend they are 'black'. If they do, the only proper connotation for them is a derogatory 'wigger' or 'putting on black face' because such pretension is just more oppression — taking the good created by the struggle of being 'black' and making it 'white'.

Actually, this logic does makes some sense as a tactic if properly used. Since their premise is that omnipresent white supremacy physically, socially, and culturally makes "black" inferior and thus American culture and society will treat 'black bodies' unjustly as a 'race' of black bodies, Coates and his worshipers conclude they must accept they are "black bodies" of a black "people", "tribe", or "race" and as a strategy of self-identity exclude anyone from being one of them who are not "black bodies" in a black "people", "tribe", or "race". If they do not watch out for each other no one will is a valid tactic used by religions, ethnicities, tribes, nations, and so forth throughout history and often is the mechanism used to create or empower the ethnicity, society, culture, and so forth in a fight against their opponents.

Of course, the difference is that for religions, ethnicities, tribes, nations, and so forth that have successfully used such a tactic, it was not their overall strategy to define themselves by it. When the various Slav tribes were so commonly taken as slaves to other parts of Europe, the Mideast, and Africa that it their identity became our word "slave", they still identified themselves by their Slav tribe before becoming slaves, while they were slaves, and after they were slaves — unless of course they adopted or were forced to adopt a different religion, ethnicity, tribe, nation, or so forth. They used their slave status as a defense tactic to continue being a Slav to give them an offensive will-to-fight or *espirit de corps* against their masters if not joining them as many did (such as the Janissaries and the Mamluks who started out as Slavic slave troops for the Muslim empires but eventually became their ruling classes), but they did not strategically define their race or personal identity by their slave identity. Such would defeat the purpose of using it as a defensive and offensive tactic. It is equivalent to saying or surrendering: I am not what my family and community say I am but what my master says I am. Doing so will not give a will-to-fight but means the fight is lost.

The downside of defining one's group identity as *solely* the oppressed of an oppressor is that losing that identity means losing one's identity. As contemplated previously, by the nature of language and ontology, there is no such thing as self-identity that is not defined by social group identity of which we can speak. Unless one has a replacement identity, there is no incentive to do lose one's identity and thus one's meaning in life to live a meaningless life — unless leading a meaningless life is one's meaning but this is a separate issue I will contemplate further on. If the only options are oppressed or oppressor that by definition means Blackness (oppressed) or Whiteness (oppressor), being an oppressed Black gives meaning to one's life as much as any other meaning unless one becomes the White oppressor. So, a Black who passes as White or who actually becomes the oppressor should by definition become White, right? Since according to Coates and his worshipers we live in a world of white supremacy in which white people are by definition the oppressors of blacks, are we able to call blacks who are the oppressors white or call them more white than most whites? "A white Congressman once said of black Congressman Augustus Hawkins, "Gus Hawkins is whiter than I am".[84] As when Toni Morrison called President Bill Clinton our first "Black President", are we able to call some whites black or more black than some blacks? Are they going to admit class trumps race?

For example, President Obama's National Security Advisor Susan Rice has led a life of prestige, privilege, and power among the Powers-that-be. She was born in Washington, D.C., of two black parents consisting of a Cornell University economics professor who was also the

---

[84] Sowell, Thomas. *Intellectuals and Race.* p. 1.

second black governor of the Federal Reserve System and an education policy scholar. She is a three-sport athlete, student council president, and valedictorian from National Cathedral School in Washington, D.C., an upper class private girls' day school, and is a graduate of Stanford University and New College, Oxford. She served on the staff of the National Security Council and served as Assistant Secretary of State for African Affairs during President Bill Clinton's second term and as UN ambassador. She is married to a white guy ABC television producer. She has two kids. Based on culture and social relations, to any working class kid such as myself she appears to be modern upper class and a very powerful member of both our modern ruling class and its intelligentsia. She is among the Powers who decide what ought to be and through the monopoly on violence that is the law would give the orders to kill me and my entire family (doubt if she would do the killing herself since new school Powers need not bloody their hands with the actual killing) if need be to keep her Inner and Outer Party in power.

Since by definition she is one of white society's oppressors of black people, can I call Susan Rice a white woman? Can I call her a white woman who happens to be black (as I usually do)? No, this would be racist because she is physically black and calling her white is racist though true according to Coates and any consistent application of the concept of Whiteness. What if she went to "Black No More" and changed to a white skin color? Is she still black? According to Coates and his worshipers' logic, the answer is yes because she was born black and thus is black and inherits the legacy of oppression, slavery, and discrimination that is being born black regardless of her being in control of whiteness. A pure social construct form of genetics.

Thus, the logic of Coates and his worshipers works both ways: under no circumstances can a white be black nor a black be white. Our technology of "White No More" and "Black No More" thus would do nothing to solve this problem. Even if skin color stopped being a genetic marker fixed at birth and became just a fashion choice and thus we could eliminate the concept of skin color 'race' and associated racism entirely to replace it with an -ism against persons who choose black as the fashion choice of skin color, all of this would still be racist. Being 'black' is a race, people, or tribe created not by skin color but by racism; it is a legacy of racism and slavery that is a birthright to all who are black. Any attempt by whites to be 'black' hijacks that legacy and is an attempt to hide it and its responsibilities (such as reparations) and is racist.

In the fabric of language used by the supposed non-racists who wanted Dolezal to lose her job, by Coates, and by his worshipers, just as with the language fabric of racists, the initial fabric tread or stitching that associated being black with skin color at some point has become disassociated from skin color. For Coates and his worshipers, for post-modernism and for social justice theory, 'black' now means a legacy of oppression, slavery, and discrimination because of black skin color by Whiteness. It is a legacy handed down from black generation to black generation as a genetic birthright regardless of the circumstances of the birth, the actual skin color, or of the life circumstances of the child. Thus, we have new school racism. This change in language tread and stitching is a substantive and essential change in the use of the words 'race' and 'racism'. If "race" truly "is the child of racism, not the father", unlike the converse situation, the father can die and we would still have the child — regardless of technology. Having race around allows for it to become a racist father itself of new school racism. The masters of the words have given "race" a new use and usefulness in the fabric of reality.

Thus, with or without race, we will have racism that in turn will create race and the self-generating perpetual cycle will continue. If there is to be Blackness, there must be Whiteness. Gutman's replacing of race with color consciousness replaces the words without changing the reality; new school racism creates a new school racism for our reality while keeping the words of the old school racism. The end result is the same: race continues to exist and continues to be used by those masters who control our normative language to create a world in their image that includes racism. Even technology for the foreseeable future will not solve racism nor eliminate the concept of race but simply change its form.

"Race is more than a biological category or a social category. It has become an industry, with its own infrastructure, branches, incentives and agendas."[85] This answers what race is in the post modern world, but how is it related to class?

---

[85] Sowell, Thomas. *Intellectuals and Race.* p. 128.

## VI. ANALYSIS / THE RELATIONSHIP BETWEEN RACE AND CLASS – PRESENT AND FUTURE

*It's tough to make predictions, especially about the future.*
— Yogi Berra

"I'll tell you what's at the bottom of it, ... If you can convince the lowest white man he's better than the best colored man, he won't notice you're picking his pocket. Hell, give him somebody to look down on, and he'll empty his pockets for you."[86] — President Lyndon Johnson. So what is going on when the likes of Gutman, Coates, Baldwin, Morrison, Appiah, and so many others who have convinced the lowest black man (and woman) that he or she through Blackness is better than the evil Whiteness of the best white man or woman? Or, is the goal to convince everyone there is no such thing as "better" or "best", that everything is equally meaningless? Class is the power to define normative language and to enforce it through the monopoly on violence that is the law upon those beneath one's class. Just as did old school racism, new school racism allows the ruling class and their intelligentsia to pick the pockets of those whom they consider beneath them because *hoi polloi* are not what they ought to be.

Only difference is that the old school politicians I saw and studied in Chicago and those that President Johnson knew in Texas and who existed for millennia throughout the era of chattel slavery and old school racism were smart enough to know what there were doing, who they were fighting, and for what they were fighting; they were also doing it in an open battle of hate with the clarity hate provides.

---

[86] Moyers, Bill. "What a Real President Was Like: To Lyndon Johnson the Great Society Meant Hope and Dignity." *The Washington Post*, November 13, 1998.

This is unlike the politicians of new school racism who have no clue as to what they are doing — even to the point of advocating self-genocide. I do not say they are evil; worse, they are just either too stupid or too self-absorbed with their moral busybody nonexistent self-identity to see their hate and thus lack the clarity it should and would provide. This is worse than evil. I have seen evil; it can be fought. Fighting moral busybodies is the equivalent of shoveling smoke. They are not evil, they just intuitively know that whatever it is they are doing, it is benefitting them by making them part of the ruling class (for the moment) and giving their lives meaning, money, and power which is all that matters — the natural human instinct for survival and for power. It is the epitome of a dialectical historical struggle of which both Hegel and Marx would be proud: because of the holistic fabric of social reality, the struggle between race and class is both a material ontological reality and a social construct of ideas so intertwined that there is no way to tell when one ends and the other starts.

This new historical struggle partially results from the death of history that is not the end of history and from the nature of our never before existent Technological Society with the power it provides us over ourselves; over others (including the Other); and over the "benign indifference of the universe" (as Camus ended *The Stranger*). As always, it is the ruling class that will control this power. What will be any resulting synthesis of this struggle?

I submit in this analysis that there are two possible general syntheses for the future, one that will result in further struggle and history and one that may not. We might get a version of Huxley's *Brave New World* that I do not see as a dystopia — it seems like a decent progressive future and we could do much worse. Or, we might get a version of Orwell's *1984* that I do see as a dystopia that might actually end history but may not. In between, there is hope in the individual virtue of empathy if it is not totally destroyed by the self-serving dribble of social justice storytelling. Historically, even real democracies and republics eventually fall into anarchy. It is only a matter of time before our fake democracy and republic does the same thus allowing for a new beginning that hopefully will not be a new form of tyranny further destroying our will to fight and to explore, discover, and conquer the universe. In addition to an analytic conceptual contemplation, I need to be a history nerd one last time.

<u>**A.**</u>        <u>**Race in the Present**</u>


Race is an industry in our Technological Society. The nature of this class controlled industry has changed from its old school past but one thing Technological Society has not changed is the substance and essence of human nature. Its dark side is better seen in microcosm, in the small insignificant activities of life or in what should be the small insignificant activity of life such as the Dolezal events than it is in major historical events macrocosm. As I learned in the Navy, if you cannot trust a sailor to clean the bilges properly you cannot trust them to properly operate a naval nuclear propulsion plant. The way new school racism viewed and treated Dolezal as a means to an end is the way it views and treats all humans which is also the way Technological Society treats all humans — as simply a means to power as an end in itself.

Dolezal is a single mother (divorced from a black man she met at Howard University) with two children. One of the children is the son of her ex-husband and the other is an adopted son. There were no accusations that she was not qualified technically or educationally for her job as head of the NAACP office in Spokane nor that she was incompetent at it. In fact, all indications were that she was good at her job. She lost her livelihood and the ability to support her family simply because — according to the Powers-that-be and their white and black friends such as Coates' black people, tribes, or black Bodies or whatever they call themselves to avoid using the word 'race' — she was not of the correct skin color. How is this different from old school racism? It is not. It is politically correct new school racism. If she was hired for the job based on her skills, competence, and qualifications, she should have kept her job regardless of her skin color and cultural, people, tribal, or whatever 'race' substitute are used to classify her. If she was hired because she was supposed to be black, be honest about it and allow everyone such freedom to hire and fire whoever they want based on their bias and prejudices — in practical reality, it is what happens anyway. If calling herself "black" was a sign of mental illness as some of the politically correct argue, based on human empathy for the misfortunes of others, this should have been just another reason to help her keep her job. The human mentality that was willing to throw her and her family into the street for having the wrong skin color is the same mentality that in the past would have enslaved her or worse for having the wrong skin color.

As seen with Dolezal, present new school racism wants a hereditary passing of power for being black in the same way old school racism wanted or wants for being white. They complement each other in a struggle for power among the members of our ruling class. The ultimate motivation for new school racism and its storytelling about oneness and the Other is power not empathy. I will tell a story myself of how empathy really works.

As I have already stated, my first six months at Harvard Law was the closest that I have come to committing suicide. What a soul crushing experience it was in addition to being mind-numbing. At one point to try to find some help I tracked down a fellow alumnus from my undergraduate school University of Illinois Chicago Circle. Before I left UICC, one advisor told me that had they had sent a student to HLS the year before and gave me his name. It was a long Polish name, something like "Wojechowskich" or worse. Since he graduated from UICC, which was a little known commuter school at the time, I though he must be a working class kid with similar life experience as me who perhaps suffered the same culture shock and could tell me how he survived. However, I could not find his name or any similar name in the HLS student list. Oh oh I thought, maybe he did not make it. I decided to check the list by undergraduate college and there I found one UICC student with a very WASP name; think it was something as basic as "John Smith" or similar. Decided to contact him anyway. Turned out he had legally changed his name. I was the last person he wanted to hear from. I was his past, he had a future. That future did not include being a "Wojechowskich" or anything to do with being a "Wojechowskich".

Good for him. I hope he made it. Hope he is a big firm law partner with plenty of upper class connections if not friends out there somewhere with a loving wife that appreciates what he accomplished in life going from "Wojechowskich" to "John Smith" — or at least has one or two hot trophy wives if the loving marriage thing did not work out. Hope he has well-educated kids with the confidence and desire to go out and discover, explore, and conquer the universe. In the end, he is only passing as upper class and will never be upper class because of his birth and past but his children will. He is only passing as upper class but that does not make him a traitor to those and the life he left behind; the whole point of the culture he left behind was to help him succeed in life not to imprison him in it. Just hope he will not forget those he left behind when the opportunity presents itself, but I do not expect him to care about his past. We can take care of ourselves as long as he and his new friends fear us enough to allow us to do so.

If he did not make it, I hope he has the strength to accept failure and find new meaning in life without demanding company in his misery.

It is empathy such as this by those that make it and those that do not make it that eliminates racism. The demands of Blackness that anyone who "passes" is a traitor to their race, tribe, or whatever, and that failure in life is to be blamed on Whiteness does the direct opposite.

## B.      The Future of Race

Race and racism is not going anywhere for the near future. If there is any old school racism around either individually or as Whiteness and Blackness, technology will eventually eliminate it through mixed births and genetic engineering that will allow anyone to be whatever color they want. However, this will do nothing about new school racism. Without new school racism: Coates would be just another college dropout dope head with a juvenile criminal record for beating up two teachers who no one cares about except to pity; Michele Obama would be just another corporate attorney who represented rich and powerful corporations until deciding to stop working in order to manage the household of a wealthy politician except perhaps to ride her husband's coattails into a political career *a la* Hillary Clinton while preaching that all women should be independent of their husbands; Toni Morrison would be just another feminist writer struggling to get by as a single mother; James Baldwin would be just another French man complaining about the United States. This list goes on and on and will continue with whoever takes over their positions of class power within Blackness and the job of by telling rich whites what they want to hear about those who define themselves by Whiteness.[87]

There is big money to be made in fighting racism just as there was and perhaps may still be in promoting it — at least in promoting new school racism. Eventually if new school racism's advocating of self-genocide is not successful, in order to continue as a means for power by the ruling class of Blackness, it will require self-segregation to avoid elimination by technology and lead to a similar result as the Reservations and Islands of the World State of *Brave New World*.

The advocated self-genocide is proceeding well. Not only are black males continuing to kill each other as previously noted; black families are disappearing with 70% of black children born to single mothers[88]; and

---

[87] Sowell, Thomas. *Intellectuals and Race.* pp. 128 - 139.

[88] Hymowitz, Kay S. "The Black Family: 40 Years of Lies Rejecting the Moynihan report caused

abortion continues to be four times more likely for Black women who are approximately 36% of all abortions in the U.S. while they make up only about 13% of the female population[89]. The latter is so successful that some University of Chicago economists are making the cold-blooded argument that abortion has reduced crime and have even given this argument a fancy name: Donohue-Levitt Hypothesis[90].

What self-genocide does not accomplish, self-segregation will. "Colleges Celebrate Diversity With Separate Commencements"[91] is a good thing? Celebrate diversity by having separate but equal graduations, clubs, organizations, resident halls, neighborhoods, and so forth? What the heck, Jim Crow without the Jim Crow laws. Should be fair and consistent and get rid of the Civil Rights laws also; if there is a right to voluntary segregate, they is no rational basis to have forced integration. Social justice race polemics will lead to the same mentality that allows American Indian Reservations to continue to exist and operate: individuals pretending to be Sioux, Navajo, or whatever dead culture and language they want to pretend they are so that a few self-centered leaders can call themselves Tribal Chiefs with power over a small fiefdom of delusional lives. If one sees a future benevolent police state as a necessary good, such waste of lives and resources on new school racism is probably harmless in the end just as the

---

untold, needless misery". *The City Journal,* Summer 2005. https://www.city-journal.org/html/black-family-40-years-lies-12872.html

[89] Morbidity and Mortality Weekly Report, Vol 66, No SS-24; 1-44. Center for Disease Control and Prevention, November 24, 2017.

[90] "Abortion and Crime, Who Should You Believe?" http://freakonomics.com/2005/05/15/abortion-and-crime-who-should-you-believe/

[91] N.Y. Times, 2 June 2017. https://www.nytimes.com/2017/06/02/us/black-commencement-harvard.htm

lives and resources wasted on maintaining American Indian Reservations are fairly harmless if one does not care about the lives wasted.

However, if one wants to minimize (I do not believe it is possible to avoid it entirely) as much as possible the adverse effects and power of a benevolent police state so that it does not become the dystopian *1984* of George Orwell, this new school racism and its destruction of the human spirit and the wasted spiritual, mental, and economic struggles it causes are just as much a physical threat to humanity's survival in its struggle with nature as was old school racism.

The *Brave New World* option is much better and is not a dystopia.

The voluntary segregation and its creation of *Brave New World* Reservations is not necessary a bad thing, and if segregation is voluntary it is not something to be pitied. The Reservations give their inhabitants meaning in life in *Brave New World* and can do so for any person willing to give up hope for meaning. Being a victim and living in the past gives meaning to one's life and serves as an explanation of all its problems and is in many ways better than hope as a source of meaning in one's life. The anxiety of hope and the depression of hopelessness are two sides of the same coin. Modern existential philosophy is proof of the power of hopelessness to give meaning to one's life. According to the philosopher Robert C. Solomon in Chapter 3 of the philosophy movie *"Waking Life"*, the existentialist philosopher/guru Jean Paul Sartre stated in an interview "he never really felt a day of despair in his life". (Based on his life of catering to Marxist and Stalinist intelligentsia and his disdain and nausea of "bourgeois" materialistic and capitalist society despite it having allowed him a life of leisure to sit around and complain about the bourgeoisie while creating no useful solutions for his complaints, it is doubtful Sartre ever knew any existential despair. Thus, Sartre had no business giving out advice such as "life begins on the other side of despair" or that "the absurd man will not commit suicide; he wants to live, without relinquishing any of his certainty, without a future, without hope, without illusions … and without resignation". What a jerk.) Sartre would be very happy in the Reservations of the *Brave New World* or in any of its Islands living in a self-centered view of the past with no hope for the future — as would all his followers (worshipers) and the followers of new school racism. These chiefs will happily double as shamans.

The same would be true of life for the inhabitants of the Islands of *Brave New World*: a lifetime spent as artists and Nietzschean creators of meaning searching for a nonexistent self-identity and the never-ending search for oneness and for the Other — that in actual practice is simply narcissism. Life may end with a whimper instead of a bang, but so what?

I first realized the power of defining meaning in life based solely on one's reflection defined as aesthetics when as a student at Harvard I went to visit the art and architecture classroom buildings. They are easily found because they are the ugliest buildings on campus. The insides are worse: the original dull white paint of the walls had long ago turned into a dirty, peeling, bruised, dusty white that for some reason no one is ever concerned about repainting colorfully or even in the original white. There was dirt, dust, and trash everywhere because I assume the artists left their maids at home. The broken and haphazard furniture and other interior furnishings match the dirty and cracked walls and ceilings. Many areas smell of dust and mildew. I felt more aesthetic beauty standing watch in the battleship grey engineering spaces of a US Navy submarine surrounded by the physical beauty and harmonious music of machinery than standing in any hallway or room of Harvard's architecture and art classes. The only items in the buildings or classrooms that had any resemblance of beauty were the art in any given student's work area — which is all they cared about. Some of it was really beautiful art. Much was not. It did not matter because the individual who made it considered it art that is pretty much the foundation for the modern art world — if your rich people are willing to pay big money for it, it must be art regardless of how ugly it is. The power of the patrician class existentialism of the intelligentsia: the whole world could be a dirty, smelly, dusty, chaotic, falling apart mess but none of that matters as long as the art a few inches in front of the artist's face is pretty. The Islands will also be a happy place of voluntary segregation away from *hoi polloi*.

Unless killed off by technology or its own self-genocide, the future for Blackness and Whiteness living peacefully in voluntary segregated Reservations or Island areas of a *Brave New World* looks fairly happy and functional. It is a lot better than the violence and hate of the old school racism in which I grew up where we were killing each other in the streets.

I grew up with Istriani, Veronese, Milanese, Venetians, Sicilians, Abruzzi, Neopolitan, Polish, Germans, Bohemians, Irish, Lithuanian, Czechs,

Slavs, Croatians, Mexican, Dominican, Hispanic, and many more, all living in the same community; they all hated each other but they were all there. They were united by only one goal: obtaining the American Dream so they could move away from the Other with whom they were competing to survive. Now in our supposedly more diverse and multi-cultural society, our diversity is down to two: Whiteness and Blackness with Blackness defining itself as the oppressed of Whiteness thus there really is only one. Since this segregation of the future will be voluntary segregation, it will be a happy one while also having the clarity of hate provided by the forced segregation of the past. This is not a bad result or future given the past, much better than the *1984* option that would involve forced segregation.

**C.**        **The Present of Class**

Class is what it is and what it always was: the degree by which any individual in a social group or by which subgroups of individuals in a social group have the power to control the normative language of the entire group — it is the power to decide what the entire group normatively ought to be or do. Class is the power to decide ethics. As such, class controls the use and usefulness of race now as it always did. It is the class struggle that creates the new school race industry and its new school racism to maintain the ruling class in the same way class struggle created old school race and its racism. For this contemplation to progress in anyway, I must further contemplate one specific attribute of nature of language that is one-half of its meaning: its usefulness. Coates is definitely a genius poet as poetry is defined by the philosopher Nietzsche: "the art of creating ripples in shallow water to give the impression they are deep." Not many other college dropouts become millionaires simply by playing with words to make them useful for his needs. Such genius serves the interests of the poet to confuse and to obscure the actual usefulness of words which is what I am trying to avoid.

Studying language is difficult because we are using language to study language and thus we face conceptually the same problem as the "observer effect" of science: do our words affect the words we are studying? To get around this observer effect, we cannot limit ourselves solely to the use of reason as a tool for contemplating the words 'race' and 'racism'. Philosophy of language does give us two truths: there are existentialist words in which the meaning of words is the speaker's existence; there are non-existentialist words in which the meaning of words is their use and usefulness. An example of the former is, "I think therefore I am"; "I am therefore I think"; "I am. Therefore, I want more than just to exist". Examples of the latter are the remaining semantics and syntax of language in all its forms be it signs, words, mathematics, or whatever humans use to enforce their will upon reality. To get around this observer effect, in addition to reason, we must use understanding, imagination, creativity, analogy, fiction, and most importantly empathy. "Whereof one cannot speak, thereof one must be silent" applies to reason not to understanding, imagination, creativity, analogy, fiction, and most importantly empathy despite they're all being intertwined in our fabric of knowledge. Also, we must keep in mind Ockham's Razor to contemplate any set of truths given by any of these wordgames to avoid the unavoidable consequence of the observer effect if ignored: generating words solely for the sake of generating words. In this contemplation, we must use all these available rational and irrational tools to achieve an understanding of race and class: its reality and its created reality of words.

The meaning of non-existentialist words is not only their use but also their usefulness to that use. Regardless of what philosophy of science may conclude about science in general, in relation to class and race, science is an instrumentalist technique for predicting future experience based on past experience. Ultimately, "[s]ince all models are wrong the scientist cannot obtain a 'correct' one by excessive elaboration. On the contrary following William of Occam he should seek an economical description of natural phenomena. Just as the ability to devise simple but evocative models is the signature of the great scientist so overelaboration and overparameterization are often the mark of mediocrity"[92]. Popular culture forgets or ignores that genetics or DNA is based on statistical generalization, it only gives probabilities or very sound and valid stereotypes not certainty. So, for example, when biologists for a popular audience say that changes in DNA result in evolutionary changes in life, they are not and cannot say there is a cause and effect relationship between DNA and any changes in life nor can they even say there is a correlation between certain DNA and life because there is rarely if ever a direct correlation between a single gene and a single physical feature. Biologists do not even know whether DNA changes individual physical characteristics or whether it is the other way around.[93] When some physical characteristic beats the odds, it is called a "mutation" and they recalculate the odds and call it new DNA or genes. The exalted DNA "explanation" is quickly "becoming epistemologically vacuous"[94] with

---

[92] Box, G.E.P. (1976). "Science and Statistics". *Journal of the American Statistical Association, Vol. 71* (No. 356), pp. 792.

[93] See note 70.

[94] Buchanan, Anne V.; Sholtis, Samuel; *et al.* p. 19.

genes defined or equated by some biologists as no more than the mathematical algorithms or computer subroutines used to correlate the massive amount of data for physical traits with the equally massive amount of data that makes up DNA[95].

The ruling classes turn 'race' used solely as a scientific word into 'racism' when the existentialist reality of words gets involved. "I am. Therefore, I want more than just to exist"; we then start fabricating "ought" statements from the non-existentialist words. This is true for all of us including the ruling class. We want control over our lives and over the reality out there that is not our lives and that is always trying to control us and will eventually kill us. We see a "high frequency of certain genetic diseases" among a "population" or "race" of "Ashkenazi Jews" and we want to predict, treat, or get rid of those diseases for the obvious reason they are a threat to personal and social health and prosperity. As a result of the present quantitative availability of medical science, this usefulness of the words 'population', 'ancestry', 'race' is not used by the Powers-that-be for arguing elimination of the Ashkenazi Jew as it was in the less technical and scientific past that resulted in the present evil connotations for the word 'race', but they just as easily could if it was in their interest to do so.

The qualitative aspect of those in the ruling class who create words such as 'race' has not changed: a will to power. I have to give credit to Nietzsche for being right when he made the will to power the driving force of reality. "GOD IS POWER"[96]. For most of humanity, this will-to-power is simply a will to survive but as one rises in class and thus gains the normative power to control what ought to be, that is as one becomes ruling class, the will-to-power becomes a striving for achievement, ambition, and a striving to reach the highest possible power in life: power as an end in itself. For the highest class, the will-to-power becomes an end in itself as there is nothing else for which to will. The difference between the vast majority of humanity and the ruling class is the Powers' desire and ability to enforce their will for power upon those with less power — the monopoly on violence that is the law.

---

[95] Gerstein, Mark B.; Bruce, Can; Rozowsky, Joel S.; *et al.* p. 671.
[96] Orwell, George. *1984.* p. 277.

In using my hypothetical technological scenario and the Dolezal events to get a better understanding of human nature in general, I tried to be clear and honest as to the pragmatic nature of technology, of the factual reality of the Dolezal events, and of what is at stake. Technology has been a good for humanity in almost any way that can be quantitatively measured. As described in Azar Gat's book, *War in Human Civilization*, as a result of the industrial and technological eras, material prosperity and progress in human civilization are no longer zero sum games requiring one's tribe, city, nation, or whatever may be our social group to take forcibly wealth from another's tribe, city, nation, or whatever in order to progress materially. For the major social players in life now consisting of nation states, there is a power surplus and power interrelations making war unnecessary among them. In fact, war is no longer the best means for achieving power; peace with its sophisticated propaganda techniques and the law as a secular religious monopoly on violence provides the simplest and easiest techniques for the few to achieve power over the many. For the present, war is an option for relations between nation states and failed nation states but not between successful nation states. Eventually war will exist solely between a world-nation and "super-empowered angry men"[97] — and women if sexes continue in the future — terrorists, fanatics, zealots, just plain crazy, and the like.

This material progress results from humanity's struggles to fight and to end the wars of the past and from humanity's struggles and war with nature to survive it and to conquer it. There is still much of nature out there to be conquered. There is a whole universe waiting to be discovered, explored, and conquered. It is not clear that the new school nature of war as a struggle between a world-nation and the individual will provide the same necessary mentality, skills, and desire to conquer nature as the old school wars have done. No matter how wrongly glorified the state of war may have been in the past, workers were always able and willing to change loyalties to whatever 1% won or loss the war as necessary to survive onto the next war; in order to survive there was no getting stuck in the past for workers. Historically, lawlessness is usually the only means by which *hoi polloi* can affect in any meaningful way history.

---

[97] Gat, Azar. *War in Human Civilization*. p. 644.

Anarchy is not as anarchic as the ruling classes want us to believe, according to many economists *"anarchy works better than you think"[98]*, it simply does not work better for purposes of being a ruling class. For workers, anarchy is often better than law and order.

For example, it only took approximately 15,000 Vandals to conquer successfully Imperial Roman North Africa with a population of about three million[99] including the City of Hippo causing the patrician St. Augustine to warn of a coming apocalypse. The reality most likely is that few of the three million noticed a difference between Roman law and Vandal rule: all the tax collectors and local politicians remained the same and their lives went on as before. The apocalypse occurred for the Powers at the top — including St. Augustine — who lost their monopoly on violence to enforce their norms to a new set of Powers. The plebeians were unconcerned just as they were with the fall of the Roman Republic. The same is true for the entire falsely promoted Dark Ages of the law when the Roman Empire fell. The Visigoths who finally ended the Roman Empire conquered Rome and the Italian Peninsula of 10 million people with a land area of 800 hundred thousand square kilometers through use of a 20,000 to 30,000 strong military forces.[100] Again, it is doubtful whether any of the 10 million noticed a difference in their lives between Roman law and the Visigothic supposed barbarism except for the Powers who simply moved to the East.

However, Technological Society is now making even lawlessness and anarchy useful to maintaining ruling class power instead of threatening it. The Boston Marathon bombings and its  effects upon the community that I personally witnessed are a good example of this future state of war. Two nuts blow up the Boston Marathon eventually causing 5 – 6 deaths and approximately 265 injuries. In the aftermath, thousands of police officers using millions of dollars of equipment and earning millions of dollars of

---

[98] Leeson, Peter T. *ANARCHY UNBOUND, Why Self-Governance Works Better Than You Think.* Cambridge University Press: NY, NY (2014). p. 1.

[99] Wolfgram, H. <u>The Roman Empire and its Germanic Peoples</u>, p. 193.

[100] *See* n. 39.

overtime pay shutdown Boston and the surrounding communities and are allowed freedom to search whoever, wherever, and whenever they want. No one complained then or since about that temporary police state — seen both then and now as benevolent and as a pragmatical good necessity.

Crime statistics are all over the place for the obvious reason that no one has any incentive to honestly admit to crime or their success in stopping it — neither the criminals nor the police. Growing up, we pretty much placed cops and criminals in the same category: something like the plague to be avoided. I remember cops as being the kid bullies who grew to be the older criminals who were smart enough to understand the value of a secure government job and thus switched sides to become cops. Why anyone would expect a police officer to be fair or expect to get away with disobeying or giving grief to one pointing a gun at you is beyond me. The one time I was in a fight with a black man, when we heard sirens, we both bolted and did not wait for justice to find us as neither of us expected any. Violence was a part of life. Expectations have changed. During my 25 years of practicing law, I tried to keep track of various crime statistics. During the last few years, there were approximately 10,000 to 14,000 murders a year in the United States. Sadly, most of these murders have gone unsolved. The exact numbers are unclear because large urban areas such as Chicago, New York City, and even Gary, Indiana, have stopped reporting their homicide arrests to FBI statisticians, apparently out of embarrassment. In a bad year, an urban area such as the city of Boston and Chicago solve about 40% their murders; in a good year, those percentages go up to about 80%. In a bad year (2012), Detroit solved only 9% (34 out of 386) and New Orleans solved only 15 out of its 193 killings in 2012.

Given our rising expectations for the quiet peaceful life, it is only a matter of time before the temporary benevolent police state of the Boston Marathon bombings becomes the norm in order to control the nuts and to eliminate the remainder of the chaos and disorder caused by individual criminals. Even *hoi polloi* want such a police state despite the fact that each one of us unknowingly commits three felonies a day[101]. The reality of the

---

[101] Silverglate, Harvey. *Three Felonies A Day: How the Feds Target the Innocent.* Encouter Books (2011).

majesty of the law is that the government and its police can get any one of us and destroy our lives any time they want — it is just a question of if they want to get us.

I am not saying this is good or bad; it simply is. This is the present of class power that must be accepted to try to understand what the future of class power and struggle will be.

<u>**D.**</u>        <u>**The Future of Class**</u>

In a 1990 article, the economist Francis Fukuyama predicted the "The End of History". In a 2011 editorial, *The Economist* predicted "The End of the End of History". When capitalist economists start becoming Hegelian, something must be up. Not sure what.

As much as I hate giving Marxism credit for anything, its conclusion that "[t]he history of all hitherto existing society is the history of class struggles" was right on point. From the Plebeian Conflict of Orders to the replacing of chattel slavery with wage slavery to the labor strikes of the 19th and early 20th Century and onto the civil rights battles of the 60's, a better future for anyone who was not in the ruling classes was achieved only through violence that the ruling classes could not control and therefore whose demands they had to grant. The law and ethics have never been on the right side of history and will never help anyone except the Powers-that-be and their lawyers — who are just an intellectual proletariat but are too dense to admit it. Ethics is ruling class ideology; the law is the monopoly on violence to enforce ruling class ideology. We are surrounded by laws and ethics that by definition serve only to maintain ruling class ideology as post-modernism and social justice theory admits, but who then hypocritically ignore this truth to establish its own ruling power. The more law and ethics control us, the more we are controlled by class power. Only when the morality of struggles for power outside the law and ethics are on the right side of history and when they are lucky enough for their morality to be an idea whose time has come is any material progress achieved. Upon success, that morality then becomes law and ethics — restarting the historical cycle of class struggle that is history. As the song goes, "meet the new boss, same as the old boss".

Class struggle in the form of violent revolution and any violence is no longer possible. Even the suggestion of such leads to further technological Orwellian *1984* power for the Inner and Outer Party and its O'Brien's. Maybe that is not so bad. After all, as the bullet entered his head and he went to his grave, Winston "had won the victory over himself. He loved Big

Brother".[102] Again, I am not preaching about the good old days of struggle and battle against the Powers. Those that so preach are usually the equivalent of those that preach "money will not make you happy" or "money is not everything" — they preach this because they not only have it but have much more than those to whom they are preaching. God is power; normatively, if you win the victory over yourself to find peace in God, this is not a bad ending for one's life. "It is better to rule in hell than to serve in heaven" is nice propaganda for those who want to rule or who are destined to rule hell but not for those who do not or who are not destined to rule it.

The ruling class is supposed to provide the leadership and discipline needed for humanity's ultimate opponent in life: the antagonism and meaninglessness of the universe to our existence. This includes the ruling class of the *hoi polloi*, Plebeians, the Middle, and the Low when their time for successful struggle has arrived. However, the will and unity to fight of those  not in the ruling class are supposed to assure the ruling class does its job and does not just seek to be in power as an end in itself and become traitors to our survival.

A will to fight the struggle requires more than just an individual will that can be easily beaten, it must be a community will.   As anyone with any military experience or with any military history experience will tell you, even a pack of dogs can kill a well trained and equipped warrior if they work together. Class struggle means class struggle not individual struggle. But, it seems individual struggle may be the only future option because all forms of community are disappearing: family, race, tribe, ethnicity, nation, religion, and even socially defined sex and gender are rapidly becoming illegal forms of unity and will soon disappear. They are disappearing except for the forced unity created by government and its law that are what the lower classes are supposed to be fighting. With the disappearance of these old school means of creating a community strong enough to engage in class struggle, what will remain?  Will they be replaced by new school forms of community or by a future of isolated paper-cutout wage slaves leading homogenous lives with only an approved diversity of beliefs or opinion willing to follow orders, do what they are told, and not make trouble for the Powers under threat of becoming even more isolated outcastes? As we leave our wage slave jobs, will we build a community by uniting with the Other through acceptance of

---

[102] Orwell, George. *1984.*

our purely individual self-identified oneness — neither of which exist in reality? According to storytelling about oneness and the Other, even assuming such exist, they are a means of finding peace not of the will to fight the Other when it is trying to kill us or some other Other, so I do not see how it will create and maintain the will to fight necessary for the class struggle to continue and thus for history to continue.

I do not see any of this transition into isolated individuals lessening. As I wrote in *Why Tolerate Law?*, Christianity sold out to the power of law a century ago and is no longer a unifying equal normative opponent to the law and its ruling class as it has been for the last two thousand years of Western Civilization — in fact, as it led to the creation of Western Civilization. I do not know about women, but as sexbots and virtual reality girlfriends and wives become more realistic and accessible, men will be marrying even less then they are now. I have never been divorced, and when I was an attorney I avoided handling divorce cases as I would the plague but even with my limited experience I know a marriage that ends in divorce is to be avoided and not worth the risk of success in marriage for any conscientious hard-working man. Having a 40% chance of marriage ending in divorce is the equivalent of having a 40% chance of your parachute not opening during a sky jump. As test tube babies become the norm, marriage will further decline and single parents or no parents but a government parent will become the norm as it has for Blackness. Fatherhood is no longer considered a mandatory requirement for being a man and neither is motherhood for being a woman. Without such cultural respect and demand, both will fade away as would an old soldier. I hear a lot of complaining that professional women want to have kids at some point during their careers but in my experience their desire is similar to wanting to have the latest fashion trends; any kids produced from this need are quickly passed over to the nannies or schooling as the true parents. Having children or at least having more than one child will be limited to the rich who can afford to raise children as actual parents with nannies and the poor for whom the government can help raise by being a parent. From what I have seen of the millennial generation and the future Middle, they are more likely to raise a family of dogs than kids.

Might as well let a *Brave New World* government raise test tube babies and give them meaning in life from birth. These comments are not meant to be criticism. I am describing the most likely scenario. Upper class parents raising upper class children through nannies and other caregivers nurturing them for power from an early age have been the norm from the Ancients to Churchill, Roosevelt, the Kennedys, the Bushes, and even the Clintons. Only difference now is that Americans pretend this is not the norm, this delusion needs to disappear and will.

Again, the good old days of loving families raising loving kids were not that good — either for the parents or the kids. Love and hate are two sides of the same coin; cannot have the first without the latter. No one seems to want hate in their lives anymore so we will have to do without love. As a character on the series *Prime Minister* said, "the history of the world is the triumph of the heartless over the mindless".

The *Brave New World* option is more likely and better for our future than any *1984* option because it would be a functioning society that could go on to discover, explore, and conquer the universe and perhaps transition into something better. "His Fordship" Mustapha Mond is at least still human and thus can be fought. The Party of *1984* is God; there is no fighting it. Happiness and peace can be found in either; it is only a question of whether to end history by accepting subservience to God or continue it to see if we can do better than God.

Plato became history's first known sociologist by studying the rise and fall of governments to develop a descriptive and interpretive theory that has yet to be falsified by time: all states begin with kingship then evolve into timocracy or plutocracy; then oligarchy; then democracy; then anarchy; finally tyranny to then begin anew with kingship. According to one of the founders of our Republic:

> Remember, democracy never lasts long. It soon wastes, exhausts, and murders itself. There never was a democracy yet that did not commit suicide. It is in vain to say that democracy is less vain, less proud, less selfish, less ambitious, or less avaricious than aristocracy or monarchy. It is not true, in fact, and nowhere appears in history. Those passions are the same in all men, under all forms of simple government, and when unchecked, produce the same effects of fraud, violence, and cruelty. When clear prospects are opened before vanity, pride, avarice, or ambition, for their easy gratification, it is hard for the most considerate philosophers and the most

conscientious moralists to resist the temptation. Individuals have conquered themselves. Nations and large bodies of men, never.   — John Adams, *The Letters of John and Abigail Adams*

As a stated earlier, Technological Society may break this cycle because of the power of surveillance it gives to both the anarchy and the tyranny stage and thus its ability to negate the power that anarchy gives to the lower classes to fight the ruling classes. In a *1984* society, Technological Society reaches perfection and the individual will-to-power of the ruling class Party reaches perfection as an end-in-itself.  Its O'Brien does not seek happiness, he is beyond such trivialities in the same way God is beyond it; He exists solely to exist, existence is its own power.  However, in a *Brave New World*, the Resident World Controller Mond, and his World State motto of "Community, Identity, Stability" are still human not gods. Their goal is lasting happiness. As O'Brien and the gods of the Party knew and Winston finally understood, lasting happiness is achieved only by putting a bullet in your head the moment you finally achieve the only lasting happiness and love without hate there is in life:

He gazed up at the enormous face. Forty years it had taken him to learn what kind of smile was hidden beneath the dark moustache. O cruel, needless misunderstanding! O stubborn, self-willed exile from the loving breast! Two gin-scented tears trickled down the sides of his nose. But it was all right, everything was all right, the struggle was finished. He had won the victory over himself. He loved Big Brother.[103]

Thus, unlike in a *1984* society, at least some of the test tube babies of *Brave New World* will at some point stop being happy and want more. There thus begins a crack in the dike.

Because of the necessary presence of class in human society, it takes but a few within the Powers to create change either for good or for bad.

On the one hand, as an example of the bad, during World War II in the ratio of guards to prisoners in both legal at the time extermination and legal prisoner of war camps, it only took about a dozen armed guards to

---

[103] Orwell, George. *1984*. p. 298.

march 5000 - 6000 prisoners legally to their death camps. This is true regardless of whether the prisoners are civilians going to extermination or work camps; harden soviet soldiers marching west to German prisoner of war camps; or battle-harden German soldiers after the Battle of Stalingrad marching east to Soviet POW camps. Unfortunately, to my knowledge no one has done any statistical study on these ratios and I base my figures on my reading of World War history books, but my figures can be confirmed by any World War history book that has any such figures within it.[104] Further, the camps and any extermination process at the camps could only be operated with the help of the prisoners themselves or the entire imprisonment and extermination process would have collapsed. According to the testimony of Rudolf Hoess, Commandant of Auschwitz, the entire concentration camp system consisting of thousands of camps and the extermination of six million was operated by 45,000 SS and regular military personnel.[105] Consistent with the Natural Law of the universe, the greatly outnumbered guards chose the strongest and the healthiest of the condemned, prisoners, and POW's to assist them in killing the remaining majority.[106] In addition, as is true of all genocides throughout history — even those occurring before the word "genocide" was created to describe the events — modern genocides occurred with the knowledge of the majority of individuals and society whose law and religion allowed the killers do their killing for them.

[104] *See generally*, "Ordinary Men: Reserve Police Battalion 101 and the Final Solution in Poland" by Christopher R. Browning (Harper 2017); "Prisoners of war (World War II)" by Ronald H Bailey (Time-Life Books 1981).

[105] http://law2.umkc.edu/faculty/projects/ftrials/nuremberg/hoesstest.html

[106] http://www.law.umkc.edu/faculty/project ... stest.html; "Between 1933 and 1945, Nazi Germany established about 20,000 camps to imprison its many millions of victims." https://www.ushmm.org/wlc/en/article.php?ModuleId=10005144

On the other hand, as an example of the good, it only took the unjust execution of one innocent Orwellian Middle to allow his twelve followers to give us *The Greatest Story Ever Told* and to give the *Pax Romana* its greatest legacy: Christianity. This story about one person Jesus Christ eventually brought down the Brave New World of the Roman Empire to start Plato's regime cycle again to reach eventually the United States version of democracy.

As our United States democracy fades into anarchy, what happens next is unknown.

*The more corrupt the state, the more numerous the laws.*
— Roman historian Tacitus.

Before I reach my conclusion, I want to say that I did not mean to pontificate in this essay when getting away from a analytic contemplation of race and class to rely on personal experience, and I do wish I could end it in the Rawlsian way Appiah ends his "Race, Identity, and Culture" essay in *Color Conscious* by comments such as: "the fruitful imaginative work of constructing collective identities for a democratic nation in a world of democratic nations"; "work that must go hand in hand with cultivating democracy here and encouraging it everywhere else"; "the fundamental moral unity of humanity". Such talk is easy to spit out when one's life experience is limited to a sheltered upper class and academic life such as the life of an Appiah and that of so many others in the post-modernist and social justice movement who, as we used to say in the military, can talk the talk but not walk the walk. The social justice movement while criticizing all other prophets for hypocrisy is not bothered by the hypocrisy of their prophets such as Foucault who lived comfortably through Vichy France so that later he could lecture for others to fight the powers and to do his killing for him or by Heidegger who remained an ardor Nazi until his death in the 1970's. As I quoted Herman Melville previously, those who talk hard things think they understand hard things. They do not.

Before I go to my concluding section, I do want to add some warning about hard things that I do understand not just talk about that unfortunately may be considered pontificating and that do not lead to feel good endings. I have lived in all classes of society and have dealt with, worked with and alongside, and even physically fought with all races in addition to fighting economic battles to survive. I made it to Harvard Law as a white working class emigrant kid who was the first in his family to graduate grammar school, high school, and college; as an enlisted veteran; and as a graduate from a public university who paid his way through college and law school either by the G.I. Bill or by work. I was not admitted to HLS by my connections, as a legacy, or through affirmative action but by Class Honors and Departmental Distinction grades in college achieved by studying year round; by graduating in 2½ years despite it taking the average student four years to graduate and the genius Coates not being able to do it in five years; and by scoring high enough on my LSAT to get the attention of someone that mattered. I graduated with a B average from HLS without ever going to class after the first semester except for registration and finals. (Another attorney I know, spent his third year in California with his girlfriend; he came back only for finals and graduation.) Thus, I submit I am not as academically dumb as most people think I am. Furthermore, after graduating, I practiced as a solo practitioner trial attorney representing the dredges of society and made a good living at it up despite my battles always being against the government, large firm attorneys, and their chosen judges in which I was always out-manned, outgunned, and underfunded. I am not as dumb as most think.

Regarding education, my 2½ years studying at UICC were probably the best years of my life despite the fact that I was living and studying in my parents unheated basement with no money except for working between terms and what I was getting from the G.I. Bill. After my discharge from the Navy, UICC felt like a rebirth and a second chance at life that I squandered by going to HLS. The hope I have in education is hope given to me by illiterate parents whose intelligence was hidden by their lack of education; to my grammar school St. Frances of Rome and Fenwick High School that treated even a dumb immigrant kid such as me that barely knew what a regular bath was as a valuable soul entitled to an equal opportunity to an educated life; and to the working class commuter school that was the University of Illinois at Chicago Circle founded upon the hope provided and the social change created by the WW II G.I. Bill and that I hope still is a working class school. Harvard Law in its modern form is a monument to power as an end in itself with education being solely a means to that end. As I wrote earlier, my days at Harvard were the closest that I ever came to actually committing suicide. After all that I have endured in my life, I still find that hard to believe.

Law school is not an education, it is a fraud. I did not know that at the time and there was no one around to tell me. Before I get into the particulars of HLS, law school, and the law, as far general post-modern social justice humanities and social science education go, I have nothing to

add to what Orwell predicted would become of education in Technological
Society:

> .. And so today the determining factor in perpetuating a totally
> obsolete hierarchical society is the mental attitude of the ruling class
> itself. ...
>
> ...
>
> ... From the point of view of our present rulers, therefore, the only
> genuine dangers are the splitting-off of a new group of able,
> under-employed, power-hungry people, and the growth of scepticism
> in their own ranks. The problem, that is to say, is educational. It is a
> problem of continuously molding the consciousness both of the
> directing group and of the larger executive group that lies
> immediately below it. The consciousness of the masses needs only to
> be influenced in a negative way.
>
> ...
>
> In principle, membership [in the Party] is not hereditary. The child of
> Inner Party parents is in theory not born into the Inner Party. ... . Nor
> is there any racial discrimination, or any marked domination of one
> province by another. Jews, Negroes, South Americans of pure Indian
> blood are to be found in the highest ranks of the Party, and the
> administrators of any area are always drawn from the inhabitants of
> that area. ... Its rulers are not held together by blood-ties but by
> adherence to a common doctrine. It is true that our society is
> stratified, and very rigidly stratified, on what at first sight appear to
> be hereditary lines. There is far less to-and-fro movement between
> the different groups than happened under capitalism or even in the
> pre-industrial age. Between the two branches of the Party there is a
> certain amount of interchange, but only so much as will ensure that
> weaklings are excluded from the Inner Party and that ambitious
> members of the Outer Party are made harmless by allowing them to
> rise. Proletarians, in practice, are not allowed to graduate into the
> Party. The most gifted among them, who might possibly become
> nuclei of discontent, are simply marked down by the Thought Police
> and eliminated. But this state of affairs is not necessarily permanent,
> nor is it a matter of principle. The Party is not a class in the old sense

of the word. It does not aim at transmitting power to its own children, as such; and if there were no other way of keeping the ablest people at the top, it would be perfectly prepared to recruit an entire new generation from the ranks of the proletariat. In the crucial years, the fact that the Party was not a hereditary body did a great deal to neutralize opposition. The older kind of Socialist, who had been trained to fight against something called 'class privilege' assumed that what is not hereditary cannot be permanent. He did not see that the continuity of an oligarchy need not be physical, nor did he pause to reflect that hereditary aristocracies have always been shortlived, whereas adoptive organizations such as the Catholic Church have sometimes lasted for hundreds or thousands of years. The essence of oligarchical rule is not father-to-son inheritance, but the persistence of a certain world-view and a certain way of life, imposed by the dead upon the living. A ruling group is a ruling group so long as it can nominate its successors. The Party is not concerned with perpetuating its blood but with perpetuating itself. Who wields power is not important, provided that the hierarchical structure remains the same.

...

A Party Member lives from birth to death under the eye of the Thought Police. ... Nothing the citizen does is indifferent or neutral. His or her friendships, hobbies, behavior towards his or her spouse or lover, facial expressions, gestures, characteristic movements, tones of voice, words muttered while asleep -- all are jealously scrutinized. Not only any actual misdemeanor, but any eccentricity, however small, any change of habits, any nervous mannerism that could possibly be the symptom of an inner struggle, is certain to be detected. Endless purges, arrests, tortures, imprisonments, and disappearances are inflicted both as punishments for crimes which have been actually committed and as the systematic wiping-out of any persons who might perhaps commit a crime at some time in the future.

...

... The masses could only become dangerous if the advance of industrial technique made it necessary to educate them more highly:

but, since military and commercial rivalries are no longer of primary importance, the level of popular education is actually declining. What opinions the masses hold, or do not hold, is looked upon as a matter of indifference. They can be granted intellectual liberty because it is thought they have no intellect. In a member of the ruling elite, on the other hand, not even the smallest deviation of opinion on the most unimportant subject can be tolerated.[107]

I will now reveal a secret that lawyers, its professors, and most significantly its judges especially those with the most power such as the Supremes work constantly to hide and that they use to make law school appear to be and seem difficult: the law is what judges on any particular day say the law is. We are not governed by the rule of law but by the rule of judges. Maybe there was such a thing as the rule of law at one time when legal cases involved deciding whether Farmer A's cow trespassed on Farmer B's property but in a Technological Society in which all words are vague and all rules indeterminate, any set of facts can be made to comply or to be in violation of any rule. They all do it, conservative, liberal, or whatever. For example, in cases such as *Citizens United v. Federal Election Commission*, 558 U.S. 310 (2010) or *Goodridge v. Dept. of Public Health*, 798 N.E.2d 941 (Mass. 2003), in which the decisions total more than a hundred pages of verbiage and their interpretative literature make up a law library of further verbiage, the conclusions much more honestly with the application of Ockham's Razor could have been written in a few lines clear for all to discuss and dispute:

1)    Based on the life experience of the majority, we have concluded corporations are good for this country and deserve to be treated as fictional persons equal to real persons therefore we have decided they ought to be treated as persons for purposes of the First Amendment. Judgment shall enter forthwith. By the court.     *— Citizens United et al*

---

<sup>107</sup> Orwell, George. *1984*. pp. 207-10.

2.      Based on the life experience of the majority, we have concluded homosexuality is moral, medically not a disorder, and that homosexuals ought to be entitled to get married. Judgment shall enter forthwith. By the court.    — *Goodridge et al*

The problem with the descriptive and normative simplicity of these short decisions is that they create a simple interpretative wordgame of discourse about law that is truly democratic allowing for all in society to rationally discuss law and have a say in it as a social construct. This is the last thing the ruling class wants. The law enforces ruling class ideology by acting through violence or the threat of violence, but this honest reality is something no modern lawgiver wants law to be — or at least not appear to be. The law is the smokescreen behind which the Wizard of Oz can hide. Law school indoctrinates: "Pay no attention to that man behind the curtain!".

It takes great skill to write smoke and to shovel it but not intelligence. It is a special kind of skill. That is why future judges actually go to class during law school and endure its mind-numbing academics, they want to learn the wordgame for generating the smoke so that they can convert their personal morality and will-to-power into law. They are the bottom of the barrel of law students in terms of honest intellect and courage but are the elite of the moral busybodies who need to create a world in their image. Most humans want to be gods; most judges and law school academics want to be the gods of the gods. Politicians are minor gods because at least they must openly sell their soul to the Party to get elected. The law and the judges who are its cardinals and preachers are too cowardly to sell their soul openly. As I said previously, persons such as Coates, Baldwin, Morrison, Obama, and so forth are probably not evil just clueless, but I do not believe this is true of those who sell their soul to the law. You want to see a real life *1984* O'Brien? Attend the session of any Supreme Court, there will be usually five or more of them at work. Watch a special prosecutor like Mueller at work taking a two week job and stretching it to seven-figure income of billable hours for himself and his political connections. The law cares for no one and no one should care for it except to avoid its violence.

Law school as an intellectual graduate education could be reduced to a one year trade school program for those with doctorate degree in other fields: six months of classroom study followed by six months of clinical training. It is more of a trade school than an intellectual challenge to any intelligent college graduate who sees through its facade. If it were a trade school for professionals with advanced degrees in other fields, we would get better lawyers, better judges, and a better system of law with some semblance of justice and even some fairness.

The problem is seeing through its facade. Law school academia work very hard at hiding this reality and here starts the first fraud that is legal education upon which the law builds. For the intelligent that do not see through its facade, it is a system of indoctrination into loving Big Brother. For the O'Brien's of the Inner or Outer Party who know the wordgame and how it is played, it is their Room 101, or should I say, the Room 101 they keep ready for all of us.

As I wrote about in my separate essay *An Existential Philosophy of Law*, the fraud continues through law school and beyond by hiding that law is simply ruling class ideology. The law is not a gunman's threat but a mob of threatening gunmen. If a criminal mob or gunmen in one social group escaped to an island inhabited by another social group and took it over with a monopoly on violence, they eventually become the law of Mob Island with the mob's rules, oaths, codes of conduct, contract rules, pragmatic obligations of care, rules of inheritance, family rules of care, and rules for maintenance and distribution of wealth becoming its procedural law, criminal law, contract law, tort law, estate law, probate law, and so forth. The purpose of law school is to teach the attorneys it now spits out the social language wordgame skill of hiding what law is especially behind the smokescreen of inductive and deductive legal reasoning.

There is no need for me to get further into this issue in this essay. This Part is simply meant as a warning looking from the bottom up to any on the bottom that want to make the same climb and not fall back down as I have. Just as the law for millennia created chattel slavery, it now creates and maintains wage slavery. Technological Society has given the law unopposed power as discussed in the previous Part VI; it is this fact that gives me the most pessimism for our future. If life experience and history have not taught any person this, nothing I say will.

As I delineate in *Existential Philosophy of Law,* once any supposed "oppressed" becomes protected by the law, they are no longer oppressed.

Regardless of the nature of that law, be it civil rights or contract or patent or water rights or anything, such oppressed have either become ruling class or are being used by the ruling class to maintain its power. Law is concerned only with maintaining its monopoly on violence and its *status quo* power structure.

# VIII.    CONCLUSION



I did not intend to be pessimistic here. Humanity has survived much worse in history than a bunch of whining about race and slavery, it survived actual slavery. Class has always been here and always will be so there is nothing to survive when dealing with class, it simply is. So, if history gives any predictive value, though it is dead, there will be no end of history with Technological Society. In fact, the best possible scenario is a return to the Ancient way of admitting the existence of class and making it explicit. Now that we know class exists necessarily, we should make explicit the classes into which persons are born. I would suggest at least: 1) Patricians subdivided into true Patricians and Capitalists and their supporting *intelligentsia*; 2) Plebeians subdivided into *petite bourgeoisie*, wage slave proletariat, and intellectual proletariat; and 3) *Lumpenproletaria.* The answers to the questions with which I started are as follows:

1.    What is race:

> At present and for the foreseeable future: "[r]ace is more than a biological category or a social category. It has become an industry, with its own infrastructure, branches, incentives and agendas."[108]

2.    What is class:

---

[108] Sowell, Thomas. *Intellectuals and Race.* p. 128.

Class is the degree by which any individual in a social group or by which subgroups of individuals in a social group control the normative language of the entire group — it is the power to decide what the entire group normatively ought to be or do. In its most basic conceptual form, class is the power to decide ethics.

3.      Are class and race social constructs or ontologically real?

At present, ontology is a holistic fabric of intertwined words and facts varying from the abstraction of aesthetics, logic, and mathematics to the purely predictive instrumental meaning and facts of hard science. Race and class are intertwined threads in this fabric existing as both social and natural kinds depending on their usefulness to the masters of these words.

4.      What is the relationship between race and class?

Class is a necessary reality in all social groups. Because the ruling class controls the usefulness of all words, the meaning of race or even if it has any use or usefulness will always be a servant of class.

I was not able to reach the topic of propaganda and its relation to storytelling, hopefully I will reach that topic another day. It is a problem distinct and independent of race and class.

# EPILOGUE:
## Quantitatively Based Classes

In my book "They Hate if You're Clever and Despise a Fool", I argue social classes are an inevitable and necessary part of any society because class struggle is necessary for social progress. I end the book with proposed classes to be accepted consisting of 1) Patricians subdivided into true Patricians and Capitalists and their supporting intelligentsia; 2) Plebeians subdivided into petite bourgeoisie, wage slave proletariat, and intellectual proletariat; and 3) Lumpenproletaria. These classes are conceptually qualitative. Upon further reflection, I now understand this ending proposal to have been wrong. Recognizing qualitatively defined classes in practice only serves to tip the balance in favor of those with the power to define concepts and quality which are always the ruling classes and their Inner and Outer Party. Classes should be defined as best as possible numerically so it is evident to each person in what class they are and in what class they want to be. In addition, numerically defined classes will allow for explicit conceptualization of what obligations are owed to each class by the government and what obligations are owed to the government by each class. All language is vague including numeric language, but the vagueness can be dealt with much better through the use of quantitative rather than qualitatively defined social classes. Probably the best way to do this is by using property-based classes as was used by the Roman Republic.

I have dealt with this issue before when contemplating the use of standardized testing as a measure of education and for school admissions. The argument against standardized testing is that standardized testing favors the rich and the dominant culture because they have the resources to prepare for these tests and their culture defines the correct answers to these tests; further, qualitative methodology such as interviews and examination of life experience is argued supposedly to allow for creating and accepting diversity in a student body. This argument is nonsense in practice. In reality, all methodology favors the rich and the dominant culture regardless of whether it is standardized testing or supposed qualitative methodology. However, the advantage of standardized testing, especially for STEM subjects, is that the answers are the same for all classes and thus all are measured by the same standard. 2+2=4 for both the rich and the poor. If a poor person gets correct answers on a standardized test, they must be accepted as correct in the same way an upper class correct answer must be accepted on such test. This is not true of qualitative testing. What a hiring or admission committee wants to hear and the form in which they want to hear the answer to whatever nonsense questions they ask for diversity purposes is best known and usually known only by someone who has grown up in the upper class culture of the committee members since birth. Unlike math, such socialization is not something one can learn outside one's social class; it is something one is born into and one grows up in and into. For these non-standardized examinations, 2+2 may in fact =5 when they want it to equal 5. One knows when 2+2=5 by growing up in the social class that decides when 2+2=5 not by learning it.

As is fairly well-known, the Roman Republic was divided up into three general classes consisting of Patricians, Plebeians, and Slaves. However, through their censuses, the Republic further divided these classes quantitatively. These subdivisions though varying at times generally consisted of: Senatores owing property value of > 1,000,000 sestertii; Equites > 400,000 sestertii; Plebeian commoners of the First Order >100,000; Second Order >75,000; Third Order >50,000; Fourth Order >25,000; Fifth Order >11,000; less than 11,000 and the landless poor were considered Proles and Proletarii. These classes were used to define the representatives each class got in the various assemblies of the Republic; the votes each of their representatives held in each assembly; and the number of electors each class received when it came time to vote for the patrician senators including the Tribune of the Plebs in the Senate and for any legislation passed by the Senate. These classes also decided the required contribution of each citizen to the Roman military. For example, the Equites were called such because they were required to provide horses and cavalry; the First Order Plebeians became the famous Triarii of the Roman Army of the Republic — the Latin expression equivalent to our "when the going gets tough, the tough get going" was "time to bring in the Triarii." Even the Prols and Proletarii, as freemen, were expected to provide oarsmen for the war galleys. These economic-based classes and the class consciousness, struggle, and resilience they created transformed the failed and sacked Roman Kingdom from a tribe limited to the City of Rome and the surrounding hills to the Roman Republic conqueror of the Italian Peninsula in a hundred years and then of most of

Europe and of the Mediterranean within the remaining 400 years of its life. As always occurs, the Patrician class eventually got too powerful, overcame the power of the other classes, and the Republic became the Empire — our future unless we wake up to it.

When creating such classes, we must make sure to count gross ownership of property and economic value not net ownership — that is, we must not subtract for debt. Being in debt runs the risk of eventual failure but at least it indicates one has hope in the future and hope in society — it links one's success to the success of society and the reverse because society needs you to succeed and get its investment back at least and hopefully profit — again, there is hope there. Julius Caesar at the time of his rising to power was the wealthiest person in Rome but also the most indebted. He did this intentionally according to historians because both gave him power. His wealth gave him power directly. His debt gave him indirectly the full power of the wealth of his creditors because they all needed for him to succeed so as to profit. For the individual, having "f–k you" wealth is great but not for society. Debt is one of the ways a society builds the future and assures everyone is invested in that future and the reverse.

Not sure why I made this mistake in the book. I wrote the book more as a descriptive conceptual analysis of race and class than a normative suggestion of what they could be or should be which I do not like doing anyway. In the end, I prefer anarchy. In any anarchy, the natural class divisions based on wealth will develop on their own. The big problem is to get the power of the law away from trying to negate these natural class divisions — when the law gets involved, the end result is always the same: the Republic becomes the Empire and then its Fall.

**<u>Bibliography</u>**

A f r i c a n    A m e r i c a n    P o p u l a t i o n    R e p o r t .
http://blackdemographics.com/population/

Ancestry. https://blogs.ancestry.com/cm/12-stunning-civil-war-facts/

Antivist (Rock Music Band). Lyrics for *Bring Me the Horizon.*

Appiah, Kwame A.; Gutmann, Amy. *Color Conscious: The Political Morality of Race.* Princeton University Press: Princeton, New Jersey (March 16, 1998).

Baldwin, James. "Notes of a Native Son". *Perspectives in Literature: A Book of Nonfiction - Vol. 2.* Ed. Rosemary Cianciolo; John P. O'Malley. Harcourt, Brace, & World: Chicago (1969).

Bailey, Ronald H. *Prisoners of war (World War II).* Time-Life Books (1981).

Behrendt, Stephen. "Crew mortality in the transatlantic slave trade in the eighteenth century". *Slavery and Abolition,* 18:1, 49-71. DOI: 10.1080/01440399708575203

Ben P. Stein, Aephraim Steinberg. *No, You Cannot Catch An Individual Photon Acting Simultaneously As A Pure Particle And Wave.* <u>Inside Science</u> ( 2 0 1 5 ) ; h t t p s : / / www.insidescience.org/news/no-you-cannot-catch-individual-photon-acting -simultaneously-pure-particle-and-wave

Bettie, Julie. *Women without Class: Girls, Race, and Identity.* University of California Press, reissue edition, 2014.

Boghossian, Paul. *Fear of Knowledge: Against Relativism and Constructivism,* Oxford University Press (2006) ISBN 0-19-928718-X

Domhoff, G. William. *The Powers That Be.* Vintage Books, NY. (1979).

Box, G.E.P. (1976). "Science and Statistics". *Journal of the American Statistical Association, Vol. 71* (No. 356).

Browning, Christopher R. *Ordinary Men: Reserve Police Battalion 101 and the Final Solution in Poland* (Harper 2017).

Buchanan, Anne V.; Sholtis, Samuel; *et al.* "What are genes "for" or where are traits "from"? What is the question?" *Bioessays* (February 2009). doi: 10.1002/bies.200800133.

DuBois, W.E.B. *Black Reconstruction in America, 1860-1880.* Free Press, 12.2.1997 edition, (1998).

Bucktin, Christopher. http://www.mirror.co.uk/news/world-news /rachel-dolezal-disgraced-race-activist-5894315

Campbell, Joseph John. *The Power of Myth* video interview and dialogue between Campbell and writer/journalist Bill Moyers. http://www.butler-bowdon.com/joseph-campbell---power- of-myth.html

Carroll, Lewis. *Through the Looking-Glass.* McMillan & Co.: London. (1872)

Center for Disease Control and Prevention. *Morbidity and Mortality Weekly Report*, Vol 66, No SS-24; 1-44. November 24, 2017.

Coates, Ta-Nehisi. *Between the World and Me.* Spiegel & Grau: NY, NY. (July 14, 2015).

Civil War Trust. https://www.civilwar.org/learn/articles/civil-war-facts

Clancy, Kate. Twitter tweet at http://secondlanguage.blogspot.com/2017/05/kate-clancy-gets-james-watson-disinvited.html

Coelho, Ricardo L. "On the concept of energy: History and philosophy for science
teaching". *Procedia Social and Behavioral Sciences* 1 (2009)

Ellul, Jacques. *The Technological Society*. Vintage Books: N.Y., N.Y. (1964).

Evans, Gareth. "Can There be Vague Objects." *Analysis*, Volume 38, Issue 4. (1 October 1978). https://doi.org/10.1093/analys/38.4.208

Fitzgerald, F. Scott and Matthew J. Bruccoli, ed. *The Short Stories of F. Scott Fitzgerald*, "The Rich Boy". New York: Scribner's (1989).

Freakeconomics. "Abortion and Crime, Who Should You Believe?" http://freakonomics.com/2005/05/15/abortion-and-crime-who-should-you-be lieve/

Foley, John; E. Anne MacKay, ed. *Signs of Orality*. Brill Academic: Leiden, Netherlands (1999)

Gat, Azar. *War in Human Civilization*. Oxford University Press: Oxford (2006).

Gerstein, Mark B.; Bruce, Can; Rozowsky, Joel S.; *et al.* "What is a gene, post-ENCODE? History and updated definition". *Genome Res.* (2007) Vol. 17. doi: 10.1101/gr.6339607.

Goldman, Alvin. *Knowledge in a Social World*. Oxford University Press (1999).

Goldman, Alvin. *Pathways to Knowledge, Private and Public*. Oxford University Press (2002)

Hacking, Ian. *The Social Construction of What?* Harvard University Press (1999).

Hall, Stuart. *The Fateful Triangle: Race, Ethnicity, Nation (The W. E. B. Du Bois Lectures).* Harvard University Press, 2017.

Hartocolli, Anemon. N.Y. Times, 2 June 2017. https://www.nytimes.com /2017/06/02/us/black-commencement-harvard.htm

Holocaust Encyclopedia. https://www.ushmm.org/wlc/en/article.php?ModuleId=10005144

Hymowitz, Kay S. "The Black Family: 40 Years of Lies Rejecting the Moynihan report caused untold, needless misery". *The City Journal,* Summer 2005. https://www.city-journal.org/html/black-family-40-years-lies-12872.html

Isenberg, Nancy. *White Trash: The 400-Year Untold History of Class in America.* Penguin Books: NY, NY. (2016).

Jensen, Barbara. *Reading Classes: On Culture and Classism in America.* ILR Press, 1st edition, 2012.

James, William. *Pragmatism, A New Name for Some Old Ways of Thinking.* Barnes & Noble, Inc., 2003 edition, 2003.

Johnson, James W. *The Autobiography of An Ex-Colored Man.* Sherman, French & Co.: Boston, MA. (1912).

Kaldellis, A. (2008). *Hellenism in Byzantium: The Transformations of Greek Identity and the Reception of the Classical Tradition.* Cambridge, UK: Cambridge University Press. ISBN 0521876885.

Lareau, Annette. *Unequal Childhoods: class, race, and family Life.* University of California Press. 2nd edition. (2011).

Leeson, Peter T. *Anarchy Unbound: Why Self-Governance Works Better Than You Think.* Cambridge University Press: NY, NY (2014)

Michaels, Walter Benn. *The Trouble with Diversity*. Holt, 1st Holt paperback edition (20060.

Michaels, Walter Benn. "Autobiography of an Ex-White Man". *Transition*. No. 73 (1997).

Morrison, Toni. *Playing in the Dark: Whiteness and the Literary Imagination*. Vintage, reprint edition (1993).

Morrison, Toni. "Talk of the Town: Comment". The New Yorker. (October 5, 1998).

Morrison, Toni. https://www.theguardian.com/books/2015/apr/25/toni-morrison -books-interview -god-help-the-child

Moyers, Bill. "What a Real President Was Like: To Lyndon Johnson the Great Society Meant Hope and Dignity." *The Washington Post*, November 13, 1998.

Newman, Paul. As character Luke in film *Cool Hand Luke* (1967).

New World Encyclopedia. http://www.newworldencyclopedia.org/entry/Taiping_Rebellion

National Center for Children in Proverty. http://www.nccp.org/topics/childpoverty.html

Nobles, Melissa. *Shades of citizenship: Race and the Census in Modern Politics*. Stanford: Stanford University Press (2000).

Obama, Michelle. https://obamawhitehouse.archives.gov/the-press-office/2015/05/09/ remarks-first-lady-tuskegee-university-commencement-address

Orwell, George. *1984*. Signet Classics Penguin Group: NY, NY (1977).

Quine, Willard V.O. "On What There Is". *Review of Metaphysics* (1948). Reprinted in 1953 *From a Logical Point of View*. Harvard University Press. https://pdfs.semanticscholar.org/05f2/9bb9be63647f88897775461c18c96026cec20.pdf

Quine, W.V.O. (1951). Two dogmas of empiricism. *Philosophical Review, Vol. 60*, Part 1, pp. 35–36. doi: 10.2307/2266637

Quine, Willard Van Orman. *Word and Object*. The MIT Press, new edition edition (2013).

Roediger, David R. *The Wages of Whiteness: Race and the Making of the American Working Class*. Verso, new edition edition (2007).

Rosen, Gideon; Smith, Nicholas J. J. "Worldly Indeterminacy: A Rough Guide". *Australasian Journal of Philosophy*. Vol. 82, No.1, pp. 185-198. (March 2004).

Schuyler, George S. *Black No More*. Macaulay Co. (1931).

Schulyer, George S. *The Negro Art Hokum* (1926). http://historymatters.gmu.edu/d/5129/

Silverglate, Harvey. *Three Felonies A Day: How the Feds Target the Innocent*. Encouter Books (2011).

Sowell, T. *Conquests and Cultures*. Basic Books: N.Y., N.Y. (1998) p. 114.

Sowell, Thomas. *Intellectuals and Race*. Basic Books: NY, NY (2013).

Sowell, Thomas. *Black Rednecks and White Liberals*. Encouter Books: NY, NY (2005).

Stein, Ben P.; Aephraim Steinberg. *No, You Cannot Catch An Individual Photon Acting Simultaneously As A Pure Particle And Wave*. <u>Inside Science</u> ( 2 0 1 5 ) ;

https://www.insidescience.org/news/no-you-cannot-catch-individual-photon-acting-simultaneously-pure-particle-and-wave

Stephenson, Wesley. "Do the Dead Outnumber the Living?". *BBC News*. http://www.bbc.com /news/magazine-16870579

Strohman, Richard C. "Epigenesis and Complexity, The Coming Kuhian revolution in biology". *Nature Biotechnology*. Vol. 15 (March 1997).

Thomas, Hugh. *The Slave Trade, The Story of the Atlantic Slave Trade: 1440-1870*. Simon & Schuster. (February 3, 1999).

Thucydides. *History of the Peloponnesian War*. Chapter XVII "Sixteenth Year of the War - The Melian Conference - Fate of Melos" (431 B.C.). https://www.mtholyoke.edu/acad/ intrel/melian.htm

Salam, A.; H. A. Bethe; P. Dirac; W. Heisenberg; E. P. Wigner; O. Klein, E. M. Lifshitz. *From a Life of Physics*. Singapore, World Scientific (1989).

Shapiro, Thomas M. *Toxic Inequality*. Basic Books: N.Y. (2017).

Sokal, Alan; Bricmont, Jean. *Fashionable Nonsense*. N.Y., N.Y.: Picador (1999)

Spurious Correlations. http://www.tylervigen.com/spurious-correlations

Testimony of Rudolf Hoess. http://law2.umkc.edu/faculty/projects /ftrials/nuremberg/hoesstest.html

Trevelyan, G.M. *English Social History: A Survey of Six Centuries, Chaucer to Queen Victoria*. Longmans, Green and Co.: London (1942)

Tribus, M.; McIrvine, E.C. "Energy and information". *Scientific American*, 224 (September 1971), pp. 178–184.

Tuskegee Institute. http://archive.tuskegee.edu/archive/bitstream/handle/123456789/511/Lyching%201882%201968.pdf?sequence=1&isAllowed=y

Uniform Crime Reports. https://ucr.fbi.gov/crime-in-the-u.s/2012/crime-in-the-u.s.-2012/offenses-known-to-law-enforcement/expanded-homicide/expanded_homicide_data_table_6_murder_race_and_sex_of_vicitm_by_race_and_sex_of_offender_2012.xls

Wikipedia. "List of Wars Involving Croatia". https://en.wikipedia.org/wiki/List_of_wars_involving_Croatia

Wikipedia. "Roman Civil Wars". https://en.wikipedia.org/wiki/Roman_civil_wars.

Wikipedia. "World Population". https://en.wikipedia.org/wiki/World_population

Windschuttle, K. *The Killing of History.* Encounter Books: NY, NY (1996).

Wittgenstein, Ludwig. *Philosophical Investigations,* translation from the German by G.E.M. Anscombe. Wiley-Blackwell, 4th edition (2009).

Wittgenstein, Ludwig. *Tractatus logico-philosophicus,* translation from the German by C. K. Ogden. Mineola, NY : Dover Publications. 471st edition (1998).

Woese, Carl R. "A New Biology for a New Century". *Microbiology and Molecular Biology Reviews.* June, 2004. DOI: 10.1128

Wolfgram, Herwig. *The Roman Empire and its Germanic Peoples.* U. of CA. Press (1993).